PRAISE FOR 60 DAYS T

"If you want to use LinkedIn to its fullest potential, read this book. Full of invaluable tips and strategies, you'll learn how to leverage this incredibly powerful platform and build lasting connections."
— Dorie Clark, author of *The Long Game* and executive education faculty, Duke University Fuqua School of Business

"LinkedIn, when done right, is a game-changer. This book shows you EXACTLY how to do it right. Tremendously practical read here."
— Marcus Sheridan, bestselling author and speaker

"Ready to IGNITE your LinkedIn game? Josh drops value bombs galore in *60 Days to LinkedIn Mastery*. Read it and implement the steps and your LinkedIn game will soon be on FIRE!"
— John Lee Dumas, host of "Entrepreneurs on Fire" and author of *The Common Path to Uncommon Success*

"I thought I was already a LinkedIn power-user, until I read this book! Best practices abound for beginners and experts alike, all broken down into bite-sized actions to take each day."
— Kiri Masters, coauthor of *Amazon for CMOs* and eCommerce industry expert

"This book is a goldmine of LinkedIn strategies from some of the very best LinkedIn experts on the planet. If you've been on the fence about investing more time and energy into LinkedIn, this is the only book you need to convince you that a massive opportunity awaits you on the platform."
— Michaela Alexis, LinkedIn coach, trainer, and 3x LinkedIn Learning author

"LinkedIn is a valuable tool for those making an entrepreneurial leap, and this book teaches entrepreneurs how to use LinkedIn the right way to grow their businesses."
— Gino Wickman, Author of *Traction* and *Entrepreneurial Leap*

"I personally know CEOs with net worths in the tens of millions who have worked with Josh Steimle and have told me they never could've predicted how much his LinkedIn advice could help them grow their business. Gary Vaynerchuk constantly tells us LinkedIn is a top opportunity when it comes to social media, but he doesn't give many how-to details. When it comes to the practical steps one can take, Josh's book makes it easy and will yield an incredible return on investment for literally any business person."
— Jess Larsen, Chairman of commercial real estate fund Graystoke Investments and host of the "Innovation and Leadership" podcast

"Josh's *60 Days to LinkedIn Mastery* is a simple and powerful step-by-step guide and comprehensive checklist that will empower thought leaders to leverage the power of LinkedIn."
— Ryan Foland, Speaker, Sailor, Ginger, and author of *Ditch the Act*

"I learned more by reading this book during one weekend, than from 6 years of using LinkedIn on my own."
— Ben Ward, Founder of Forward Leadership and Author of *Sellership: How Top Salespeople Become Remarkable Sales Leaders*

"In reading *60 Days to LinkedIn Mastery*, I realized I had no strategy, or even a clear idea of my LinkedIn goals. Josh Steimle changed all that for me! Now I know my LinkedIn goals and how to achieve them. This guide, with all its practical tips, is easy to use and explains how to think like LinkedIn so you can get the maximum benefit out of the time you spend there."

— Lisa Tener, Book Coach and Creativity Expert, Author of *The Joy of Writing Journal*

"A majority of people get LinkedIn wrong. Why? Because they are in it for themselves. In order to generate long-term positive results, it's important to identify the true pain point of the person on the other side of the screen. What keeps them up at night? What causes them anxiety and stress? With those answers, anchor your service as the solution to their problems, and *60 Days to LinkedIn Mastery* is a great starting point."

— Brendan Kane, bestselling author of *One Million Followers* and *Hook Point: How to Stand Out in a 3-Second World*

60 DAYS TO LINKEDIN MASTERY

60 DAYS TO LINKEDIN MASTERY

JOSH STEIMLE

WITH VIRGINIE CANTIN, ANDY FOOTE, LORRI RANDLE,
KYLE WECKERLY, BEN WISE, & AARON WRIXON

TAFT

www.JoshSteimle.com

Published by Taft House

DEDICATION

To my wife, Brynn, without whom this book never would have been completed.

THANKS

To my coauthors, who added detail that made this book much more useful and provided feedback that kept me from embarrassing myself. My deepest gratitude.

Virginie Cantin
Andy Foote
Lorri Randle
Kyle Weckerly
Ben Wise
Aaron Wrix

To all those who supported this book with their time, feedback, and inspiration, thank you.

Lacey Abbacchi
Michaela Alexis
Michael Alf
Amir Amraie
Steve Amundsen
Christy Anderson
Clark Anderson
Derek Ardolf
Spencer Arntsen
Marcos Avila
Anke Bebber
Ling Becker
Charles Beddow
Braden Bennett
Corey Blake
Hengameh Bolouri
Jared Bradley
Greg Bray
Ian Bremmer
Chip Browne
Joe Bunting
Peter Burgess
Rob Callan
Nelson Catala
Sheelagh Caygill
Anita Chan
Wai Yeong Chan
Bryan Christiansen
Chris Cochella
Lee Constantine
Tyler Cook
Charles Coonradt
John Corcoran
Austin Craig
Aliyah Dastour
Nicole Davis
Jessica DeMartini
Gurleen Deol
Corina Denov
Falguni Desai
Sterling DeVard
John DiBenedetto
Heather Dopson
Amir Drori
Michael Eagleton
Benjamin Eckart
Nir Eyal
Ellen Feldman Ornato
Tim Fife
Ryan Foland
Christian Foucault
Greg Fox
Kyle Fraughton
Christopher Freeman
Alexandra Galviz
Allen Gannett
Barbara Gates
Matthew Gattozzi
Phil Gerbyshak
James Ghormley
John Godfrey
Stephen Greco
Tracy Griffiths
Steve Guidetti
Andrew Hahn
Deanna Hall
Joe Hall
John Hall
Blake Hansen

Eric Hanson
Peter Harris
Tyler Hartle
Val Haskell
Stacy Havener
Julian Hayes II
Judi Hays
Gay Hendricks
Josh Henkin
Brent Hicken
Mk Hicks
Chris Hogg
Chip Hopper
Adam Houlahan
Jukka Ikonen
Jason Izatt
Sterling Jenkins
Seth Johnson
Ernest Jones
Thomas Jorré
Brendan Kane
Guy Kawasaki
Kurtis Kildew
Larry Kim
Adrian Klemme
Andy Klump
Oliver Kriska
John Kruger
Christina Kumar
Jean-Pierre Lacroix
Jess Larsen
Nick Larsen
Ben Laws
Jake Leahy
Tyler Lemke
Larry Leung
Felipe Lodi
Sandra Long
Michael Maggitti
Carl Majors
Michael Maloney
Andrew Martin
Jared Mason
Brian Masters
Anna McAfee
Michael McLean
Kip Meacham
Peter Messervy
Mads Monsen
Gerard Moran
Samantha Moran
Jed Morley
Kelly Murphy
Nancy Murphy
Gregory Mushen
Sertac Mustafaoglu
Luke Nehring
Mattson Newell
String Nguyen
Steven Noe
Eric O'Neill
Lay Tin Ooi
Juergen Olbrich
Garret Orr
Michelle Payne
Adam Peek
Ayelet HaShachar Penrod
Bill Rader
Scott Rafferty
John Rampton
Steve Rankel
Peter Ransom
Azriel Ratz
Ryan Rhoten
A Riaz
Ari Rule
David Safeer
Scott Sanders
Jacob Sandler
Ken Sanofsky
Robbyn Scribner
Roberto Severino
Tom Shapiro
Mason Shaver
Mary Shores
Kelly Silvester
Michael Simonet
Todd Sirrine
Lachlan Sloan
Michael Smart
Lila Smith
Casey Sowers
Jamie Spence
Christopher Spossey
Tyler Stahle
Lawrence Steimle
Jeff Stephens
Melissa Swartz
Tao Tao
Paul Taylor
Sharla Taylor
Jeffrey Thelen
Devin Thorpe
Douglas Timms
Lee Towe
Marcia Layton Turner
Edgar Valdmanis
Margaret Valentine
Richard van der Blom
Frederique van Egmond
Doug Walker
Ben Ward
David Warren
Bev Wax
Winfried Weinhold
AJ Wilcox
David Wilcox
Itzik Woda
Timothy Wolfley
Josineide Wood
Nikki Woods
Sara Wramner
Trapper Wyman
Yunzhe Zho

CONTENTS

60 DAYS TO LINKEDIN MASTERY

INTRODUCTION

With 774 million users (as of September 1st, 2021)[1], LinkedIn is the largest professional social network in the world, and it's still growing rapidly. It isn't much of an exaggeration to say "Everyone uses it," and yet, how much value have you gotten from it?

Most people, when I ask this question, will respond, "I'm not sure . . ." because most people don't use LinkedIn to its full potential, if they use it at all. For years, I didn't, either.

Like almost everyone, I treated LinkedIn as an online resume database. I updated my profile once in a while, and every so often I'd log on to look for someone to hire or to screen a potential employee. But everything changed for me in 2013.

In 2013, LinkedIn bought the Pulse blogging network for $90M, an acquisition that gave LinkedIn users the ability to write blog posts that had high visibility through the network. At the time, I wrote weekly articles for *Forbes*, and after hearing how others were getting exposure by writing articles to publish on LinkedIn, I decided to test the system.

I copied and pasted one of my articles (following *Forbes'* guidelines for doing so) onto LinkedIn and it blew me away when it was read fourteen thousand times and received hundreds of comments. That

---

[1] See http://news.linkedin.com/about-us#Statistics. Accessed 2 October 2021.

was several times the attention the same article received on the *Forbes* website.

I repeated this process several times and LinkedIn always out-performed *Forbes* by a long shot. Some of the articles I published on LinkedIn were read hundreds of thousands of times and received thousands of comments.

Then LinkedIn pulled the rug out from under me.

ARTICLES, POSTS, AND MORE

In late 2017, LinkedIn changed its content algorithm and stopped displaying articles in the feed as prominently as before.

Suddenly, it was all about posts.

Before we proceed, let's clarify a few terms.

> **Feed:** The never-ending stream of content that shows up when you go to LinkedIn's homepage.
>
> **Article:** On LinkedIn, this is effectively a blog post. Articles may be thousands of words long and include rich text editing with pictures, graphics, links, and video.
>
> **Post:** A post is much shorter than an article—posts are limited to three thousand characters (although a few people are still limited to the former 1,300 characters). There is no rich text editing available in posts. You can upload an image or video that displays at the bottom of the post. You can also include links to content, and LinkedIn will automatically preview this content at the bottom of the post.
>
> **Algorithm:** The automatic system that makes LinkedIn work the way it works. The algorithm determines what content will show up in someone's feed and what won't. And what will

show up when someone searches on LinkedIn for a certain keyword or keyword combination. It also determines what suggestions LinkedIn will give you for who you should connect with and who you should follow.

LinkedIn's algorithm controls virtually everything you see on LinkedIn. Nobody but LinkedIn's staff knows exactly how the algorithm works, and even within LinkedIn no single person understands it all—it's too much. Rather, individual teams work on different parts of the algorithm, constantly experimenting with it, constantly making changes.

Outsiders, such as myself, combine the results of experimentation, occasional clues from LinkedIn's official announcements, and a knowledge of LinkedIn's intentions to piece together a rough working model of the algorithm.

Whenever LinkedIn changes the algorithm, marketers cry. (You won't, however, because I'll prepare you to take advantage of changes.)

Note: For a full glossary of LinkedIn terms, check out my free Ultimate LinkedIn Mastery Resource List at BlueMethod.io/list.

Getting back to my story. . . .

PURE "BROETRY"

When LinkedIn changed its algorithm to favor the much shorter posts instead of articles, I felt like I had been robbed. I was just getting the hang of articles and attracting real attention!

No matter, I concluded. One must carry on.

I began to search for information on how to succeed in the feed, and in the midst of my research, I came across a blog post by Josh Fechter detailing how he generated millions of views on his LinkedIn posts.

As I read Fechter's blog post and looked at his LinkedIn posts, I detected a certain format.

Every sentence was on a separate line.

Each sentence was short and punchy.

He would start out with something catchy, like, "It was the worst day of my life."

Then he would go into detail and tell a story.

(There was always a story.)

Then he would tie everything up in a helpful and inspiring lesson.

There were no images, no links, and no video.

Just plain text.

He also focused on getting comments, which helps make content go viral on LinkedIn. (More about this later.)

Interesting technique, I thought. A little strange, but why not give it a try?

I copied Fechter's style, not only the line spacing, but the way he crafted all his content, and voila! My posts also began to go viral and generated millions of views.

Fechter's writing style caught on and was imitated by many, and even today you see its legacy. I mastered it so well that I was featured alongside Fechter in a Buzzfeed article wherein a poetry professor at The College of the Holy Cross critiqued our work.

Fechter would go on to manipulate the LinkedIn algorithm until LinkedIn banned him for life and changed their algorithm to make it harder to game the system. Broetry fell out of favor and after my period of experimenting with it, I also left it behind . . . mostly.

As my writing on LinkedIn evolved, so did my intent. Many of my viral posts had been fun experiments, but little more. They didn't serve any other purpose than to see what worked and what didn't. If I was going to keep posting on LinkedIn, I needed a compelling reason.

I found a purpose for posting on LinkedIn when I used it to grow my marketing agency, creating content that attracted clients, partners, and potential team members.

In addition, I created an entirely separate business around LinkedIn consulting (see BlueMethod.io), and received invitations to speak at conferences and workshops. In addition, there were all the new friends and relationships I built. It felt pretty good to see such tangible success from my LinkedIn content.

There was nowhere to go but down.

YET ANOTHER CHANGE

No sooner had I enjoyed a few months of success with my posts on LinkedIn—getting hundreds of thousands of views on even my worst-performing posts—then LinkedIn changed the algorithm once again. This time, they began to funnel the vast attention of their network toward native video rather than plain text posts.

However, LinkedIn didn't kill off text posts as they did articles—as of this writing, you will still gain a respectable amount of attention with nothing more than plain text posts. If one thing is certain, though, it's that LinkedIn will change the algorithm again in the future—and, once again, marketers who have gotten fat and lazy by sticking to the status quo and maximizing short-term tricks will cry themselves to sleep.

But you won't cry—because you know that algorithm changes get rid of competition, *and* because this book will teach you how to build your foundation on long-term strategies that tweaks in the algorithm won't knock down. This book will help you, as hockey legend Wayne

Gretzky famously said (or didn't say)[2] about his success, to focus not on where the puck *is,* but rather on where it's *going.* Understanding LinkedIn's long-term strategy will help you give LinkedIn what it wants, and get the rewards it gives to those who feed it.

What does LinkedIn want?

LinkedIn wants more users, and it wants those users to spend more time on LinkedIn (because users who spend more time on LinkedIn are more likely to purchase its paid services or click on ads). If you create great content for LinkedIn, LinkedIn will reward you with attention. Let me repeat that, because it sums up what this entire book is about:

If you create great content for LinkedIn, LinkedIn will reward you with attention.

The attention will come from potential customers, partners, employees, or employers. LinkedIn launched "creator mode" in early 2021 to encourage users to continue to create more free content as often as possible, but mainly to entice new creators into the content creation system. More content means people will stick around longer on LinkedIn. (For more on creator mode, see Day 26.)

No matter what algorithm changes LinkedIn makes—as long as you help LinkedIn get what it wants, it will help *you* get what *you* want.

THE KEY TO GREAT CONTENT—THOUGHT LEADERSHIP

Since my early days on LinkedIn, I've experimented with every format and type of content. I've made all the mistakes so you don't have to.

---

[2] See https://www.fastcompany.com/40565/cdu-gretzky-puck-stops-here. Accessed 2 October 2021.

After everything I've learned, what I can say with certainty is that if you want to create great content on LinkedIn, the kind that will help you grow your business, find a job, or progress in your career, then create "thought leadership" content.

Thought leadership happens when you share useful information and knowledge based on your expertise in a certain area. When you create thought leadership content, it has the effect of establishing you as a recognized expert in your field. For example, Susan Cain, the author of *Quiet: The Power of Introverts in a World That Can't Stop Talking*, is a thought leader who discusses how we often undervalue introverted people. Steve Blank is a retired tech entrepreneur from Silicon Valley who now lectures at Stanford and is one of the most widely recognized thought leaders on building successful startups. Both Cain and Blank became thought leaders because of the content they created, which led people to follow them.

Thought leadership content is sought after by people from all walks of life, especially business executives and other key decision-makers.

According to research by Edelman and LinkedIn, 58 percent of decision-makers read one or more hours of thought leadership per week. Sixty percent of the 1,200 respondents who participated in the same survey said they use thought leadership to decide what to buy and which organizations to buy from.[3]

LinkedIn wants to attract more of these decision makers, so if you create content the decision-maker audience appreciates, LinkedIn will appreciate *you* and give you what you want to encourage you to keep creating content.

---

[3] See https://business.linkedin.com/marketing-solutions/blog/linkedin-news/2018/7-surprising-stats-about-the-underappreciated-power-of-thought-l. Accessed 2 October 2021.

However, because your content needs an audience, success on LinkedIn is also about making meaningful connections, connections with people who will consume your content.

"In real life, you make meaningful connections by spending time with people, getting to know them and bond over what you have in common," says my coauthor Virginie Cantin, a LinkedIn coach. "On LinkedIn, you make meaningful connections by putting yourself out there so like-minded people can relate to you and engage with your future content updates."

Because it's hard to make high-quality connections if you have a weak LinkedIn presence, effective thought leadership begins with optimizing your profile.

This book exists to make it easy for you to engage in these three activities, in the order that makes the most sense:

1. Optimize your profile
2. Make meaningful connections
3. Create compelling content

The book will give you sixty tips—one tip per day—each of which will take a few minutes to read, and in all but a few cases, only a few more minutes to implement.

If you invest a few minutes per day reading and implementing what you learn in this book, you will be a master of LinkedIn at the end of sixty days. You'll know more than 99.99 percent of LinkedIn users and will be making connections and creating content that brings you the results you want in your professional life.

HOW THIS BOOK WORKS

In 2013, I attended an event in Park City, Utah and heard Wil Reynolds, founder of SEER Interactive, speak on outputs and outcomes. Outputs are the things we get done, the tasks we put on a checklist. Outcomes are the results we want. It's easy to get lost in the outputs and forget what the outcome is that originally motivated us.

This book focuses on outputs, the actions to take on LinkedIn that will create the outcomes you want. However, there is danger in seeing outputs as ends, in and of themselves. If we chase likes, comments, and connection counts for their own sake, we fall prey to Goodhart's Law, which says, "When a measure becomes a target, it ceases to be a good measure." Even mastery of LinkedIn is not the final goal, but a means to an end.

The outcome you want may be more sales, a new job, or finding that new hire you need. Focus on the outcome, and you'll know how to use the tools you gain from this book to get what you want, now and in the future.

This book provides practical information that works right now and long-term tips that will work as well fifty years from now as they do today, regardless of how LinkedIn changes.

Note: Since LinkedIn is constantly changing, download my free and regularly updated Ultimate LinkedIn Mastery Resource List at BlueMethod.io/list.

In this book, sixty tips are organized into five sections.

In the first section, you'll find general tips focused on your mindset. Read these tips first.

In the last section, you'll find another set of general tips, which are only applicable once you've processed the rest. Read these last.

The middle three sections correspond to the three primary areas of activity listed above: optimizing your profile, making high-quality connections, and creating compelling content.

If you feel like a beginner on LinkedIn, read this book front to back, one tip per day. If you're closer to the expert side of the spectrum, you'll still find this book to be a helpful reference in which you can skip around, according to what you need help with.

Regardless of your level of expertise on LinkedIn, I hope you will find this book helpful, interesting, and even entertaining.

Enjoy!

Josh Steimle

P.S. A special note about my coauthors: Without help from my collaborators Virginie Cantin, Andy Foote, Lorri Randle, Kyle Weckerly, Ben Wise, and Aaron Wrixon, this book wouldn't exist. While the voice throughout this book is predominantly mine, much of the advice came from my coauthors or was substantially enhanced by their input. If there's any doubt about who the credit for this book belongs to, give it to them.

SECTION 1

CHASING MASTERY

At age thirty-three, I ran further than a mile for the first time in my life.

The next day, I ran a mile again. Then I ran another mile the day after that. The fourth day, I got out of bed and fell on the floor. My knees couldn't hold me up. Frightened, I spoke to a physical therapist.

"You ran three miles over the past three days?" he asked.

"Yes," I replied.

"And you've never run more than a mile in your life before?"

"That's right."

"When was the last time you ran at all, before this week?"

"Maybe ten years ago?"

He then explained to me that I needed to ease into it. It would take time for my muscles, ligaments, and tendons to adjust to an activity I had effectively never done before in my life. When it came to running, I was as much of a beginner as you could find.

Ten years later, I crossed the finish line of a 70K (43.5 mile) race that wound around Lantau Island, in Hong Kong. The race was on a mountain trail that went from sea level up to a three thousand foot peak and back down again, and then did it two more times. My time was one minute under fourteen hours (the goal I had set), and at the end, I felt great, like I could keep running forever. I felt like I had mastered the art of endurance running. Granted, I still had a long way to go to master it to the level others have (my friend finished the same race in eight hours), but at least I wasn't falling down.

When I began running, if you had told me that someday I would run up and down mountains and that my training runs would be marathon distances, there's no way I would have believed it. What I learned over the years is that if you take things slowly and ease into it, you can work up to almost anything.

Mastering LinkedIn is easier than mastering ultra marathons. If you read one chapter of this book each day and do the homework and extra credit, all of which should take you no longer than fifteen minutes, you'll be a LinkedIn expert within two months. When I say "expert," I mean you will learn how to use LinkedIn to get real results, and you'll know more than the vast majority of those on LinkedIn.

Just as with running, it's important to start easy with the basics, the foundational knowledge you'll find in this first section. Even if you know a lot about LinkedIn, don't skip these first lessons to jump ahead to the more tactical tips in the sections that follow. These first few tips will set you up for long-term success on LinkedIn for years to come.

Shall we get on with things? Turn the page, and let's start with Day 1 where we'll talk about your purpose.

DAY 1

FIND YOUR PURPOSE

When I started to create content on LinkedIn, I lacked a purpose. I wrote about whatever was interesting to me at the moment. Unsurprisingly, I got no results.

Many LinkedIn users are in the same boat. They don't know why they're on the network, why they spend time on their profile, or why they're posting content.

Without a purpose, they fill out their profile with whatever small amount of guidance LinkedIn provides, they connect with *literally anyone*, and they rarely post any content, if they post at all.

Contrast that approach with the executive who says, "I'm on LinkedIn because I'm about to make a career change," the recent graduate who says, "I'm on LinkedIn because I'm looking for my first job," or the entrepreneur who says, "I'm on LinkedIn because I want to sell more and grow my business."

When you have a purpose, it's easy to optimize your profile to focus on it. You know who you want to connect with on LinkedIn, and who you shouldn't connect with. You create content that appeals to the audience you want to influence. If you define your purpose before you optimize your profile, make strategic connections, and create compelling content, then magic will happen.

Maybe you already have a clear purpose for your business or career. Perhaps you've already got ideas about how to align your activity on LinkedIn with that purpose. Great! This book will help you do it even better.

Or maybe you feel like your purpose is unclear, or that the purpose you have in mind is difficult to connect to what you're doing on LinkedIn. No problem—this book will guide you through the steps to match your purpose with the actions that will produce the results you want.

HOMEWORK

Why are you on LinkedIn? What could it do for you, your career, or your business? Define your purpose, and if it's helpful, write it down or print it out and put it where you will see it every day.

EXTRA CREDIT

Each chapter of this book will include homework and an extra credit assignment. The extra credit will always be to create a post on LinkedIn. To do this, go to your LinkedIn homepage, while logged in, and click in the "Start a post" area at the top middle of the page. Then copy the extra credit post, or your customized version of it, and post it.

Post this to LinkedIn right now:

> *What's your main purpose for being on LinkedIn?*
>
> *I've been thinking about why I'm here, and here's what I've come up with . . . [insert your thoughts here].*

So that's me, but I'd love to know why you're here and how I can help. What's your reason for using LinkedIn right now?

DAY 2

BE NICE

In 2012, Google began a research initiative, called Project Aristotle, that studied 180 of their teams. The goal? To figure out why some teams were cohesive and worked well together while other teams failed.

It cost the company millions of dollars as many of their people worked for years to understand the matter. Finally, they found their answer.

What was it?

Teams work when people are nice.

Or as the report put it, teams that work well provide "psychological safety" for their members. Individuals feel like they can speak up without fear of being criticized. They feel free to be themselves and as a result, they're happier and more productive.[4]

Has anyone ever left a mean-spirited comment on one of your posts?

It's hard to take.

After receiving such a comment, some people decide they never want to post again . . . ever. Jerks and trolls are relatively easy to ignore

---

[4] https://qz.com/work/625870/after-years-of-intensive-analysis-google-discovers-the-key-to-good-teamwork-is-being-nice. Accessed 2 October 2021.

because they're unreasonable and we can say, "Forget this guy, he's crazy." But sometimes we receive criticism from friends or coworkers, and that's more difficult. It cuts deeper.

These individuals probably don't intend to offend. They may be trying to help by being frank and honest, or they might be joking but the tone is lost in their comment. But for those of us with thin skin, these comments fester and breed defensiveness and resentment.

On LinkedIn, we're all on the same team. Together, we will help each other reach our goals. But hurtful or negative comments make our team less effective.

It's difficult to be "nice" according to someone else's definition. We might believe some people are too sensitive and need to toughen up. Regardless of what we believe, if we want the benefits of a productive team environment on LinkedIn, we'll take responsibility and be as nice as we can, even when others are unreasonable.

Try it out for a month. The nicer you are, the more you'll see people engage with your content and connect with you.

It's especially beneficial to be nice when others aren't. "Their bad behavior makes you look good!" Lila Smith, a coach at Say Things Better, told me via email. "The contrast between their negative communication and your intentionally connective communication can reinforce what you stand for."

HOMEWORK

Be nice on LinkedIn.

To practice, go to your feed, find a post that looks interesting, read it, and leave a nice comment. It may be helpful, it may be encouraging, as long as it's nice. When you're done, do it four more times.

Pro tip: If you're nervous about how your post may come across and whether it will sound nice or not to others, try reading it out loud.

EXTRA CREDIT

Try posting this (or something similar) on LinkedIn right now:

> *Who has been kind to you in your professional life?*
>
> *Maybe a boss, coworker, maybe a stranger on LinkedIn. Here's my story. . . .*
>
> [tell a story about someone being nice or kind to you in a professional setting]
>
> *What's your story about someone being nice to you in a professional setting?*

Not only will this post help you to exercise your kindness muscles, as you read the comments others respond with, you'll see many examples of how others have expressed their niceness.

DAY 3

DON'T DO THESE THINGS

Before we get too far into this book, a few warnings are in order that may save you a lot of pain and embarrassment. If you want to become effective on LinkedIn, do NOT do any of the following:

1. Don't use LinkedIn as a dating website or to harass others. You would not believe how common this is. Telling a person, one whom you don't know, that they look attractive in their LinkedIn photo is a no-no.
2. Don't use a logo as your image. We want to see YOU.
3. Don't send an impersonal sales pitch as soon as someone accepts your connection request.
4. Don't take before giving.
5. Don't forget people are reading your posts—even if they don't comment.
6. Don't send spam messages to your connections.
7. Don't get into public spats on LinkedIn.
8. Don't tag people in posts unless the content is relevant to them.

9. Don't tag the same fifty people in every post, even if the content IS relevant to them.

10. Don't ask for fifteen minutes of someone's time "just to chat." Be specific about your intent.

Also, when describing yourself, *don't* use words like visionary, guru, rockstar, innovator, thought leader, ninja, wizard, influencer. . . .

These words are OK to use IF you're talking about someone *else* who is truly AMAZING. They are *not* words to use to describe yourself.

"A person who is actually an influencer, expert, or guru never has to call themselves one," Lacey Abbacchi, a LinkedIn coach, told me. "Leave that up to others to decide."[5]

It's OK to say "I want to become a thought leader," or "I want to become a programming ninja," because then you're being self-deprecating, rather than boastful.

Instead of using hyperbole when describing yourself, use facts.

- I am a speaker
- I am a paid speaker
- I am an international speaker
- I am an international keynote speaker
- I am a TED speaker

These are different ways to say "I'm a great speaker you'd love to hire," without saying it in such an awkward way.

Other acceptable terms you might include on your LinkedIn profile are entrepreneur, author, writer, programmer, designer, etc.

---

[5] Personal communication with Josh Steimle.

HOMEWORK

Check your LinkedIn profile to make sure you're using factual terms to describe yourself, and that you're not calling yourself a visionary thought leadership ninja.

EXTRA CREDIT

Post this on LinkedIn right now:

> *What's your latest LinkedIn resolution?*
>
> *Mine is to be more specific about why I want to chat with someone when I reach out to connect* [or put whatever your resolution is here]. . . .
>
> *If there was one thing you wish people would start doing on LinkedIn, what is it?*

DAY 4

FIND YOUR GENIUS ZONE

If you feel your lack of success stems from a lack of focus but you're still not sure what to focus on, chances are, you're too good at too many things, or too interested in too many things. The antidote is to find your "genius zone," a concept I first learned about when I read *The Big Leap* by Gay Hendricks. Your genius zone is key to making it easy to know who your audience is on LinkedIn and how to create compelling content for them.

To find your genius zone, first identify your expert zones. You don't have to be *The Best in the World* at something to be an expert, you only need to be good enough at it, or know enough about it, to help someone else. For example, you may think your knowledge of computers is minimal and nothing special, but compared to someone who has never used a computer, you're an expert.

Next, overlap multiple expert zones to find potential genius zones, like this:

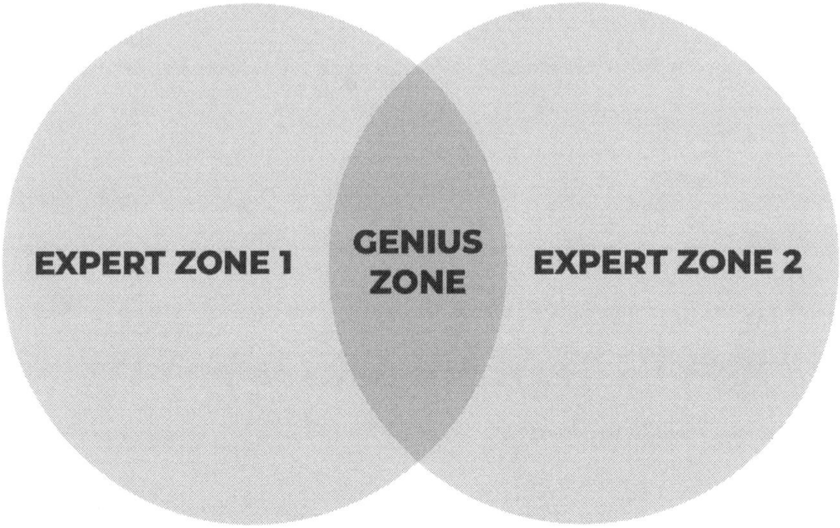

For example, my friend Dallas knows a lot about managing business operations, but by itself, that's not all that special.

However, although Dallas is American, he also speaks Chinese fluently, has lived and done business in both China and Taiwan, and on top of that, he has a track record of getting things done. If he were listing out some of his expert zones, it might look like this:

- Native English fluency
- Expert Chinese language fluency
- Multiple years business experience in China
- Multiple years business experience in Taiwan
- Strong track record of competency

Dallas could easily add a hundred more items to his list of expert zones, but you can already see how the intersection of these five expert zones makes Dallas particularly valuable to American businesses that need someone to help them do business in China or Taiwan, or to Chinese companies who want to do business in America. Your genius zone might come from combining two expert areas, or it might be three, or four, or ten.

The magic of the genius zone is that once you find it, it's easy to come up with ideas for content on LinkedIn. It's also easier to pinpoint who your ideal audience is and speak to them effectively. In addition, your service to your audience becomes more meaningful and valuable—not to mention, more fulfilling.

Note: If you'd like more detail on finding and developing your genius zone, check out my blog post at https://joshsteimle.com/influence/how-to-find-your-genius-zone.html.

HOMEWORK

Make a list of your expert zones that align with your purpose.

Overlap your expert zones to find potential genius zones.

Choose the genius zone you want to focus on that aligns with your purpose.

EXTRA CREDIT

Post this on LinkedIn right now:

> *What's your genius zone?*
>
> *I've been learning about the concept of a genius zone lately, and for me it's combining . . .* [list the expert zones that form your genius zone].
>
> *By finding my genius zone I'm able to serve better and make more of an impact in the world.*
>
> *What's your genius zone?*

DAY 5

TALK TO *YOUR* AUDIENCE

It isn't as easy to talk directly to your audience as you may think. It's especially difficult if you don't know who your audience is.

Here's a real-life example of someone struggling to speak directly to their audience on LinkedIn through their LinkedIn headline. Their headline reads:

"I help modern-day leaders develop the skill-sets of the future."

Who is the audience?

Is it leaders? To say it's modern-day leaders doesn't narrow down the field much. The audience this person has staked out is so generic they may as well say the audience is anyone and everyone.

Imagine trying to refer business to this LinkedIn user. Which of your connections would you refer? When I think of "modern-day leaders," not a single person I know comes to mind. It isn't specific enough. That means this LinkedIn user isn't going to get referrals from me, even though I'd love to help him.

Be specific.

Get clear about who your audience is (and isn't). Then, it will be easy to speak to them in language they recognize. Your posts will include only information that is of interest to this audience. Yes, that might turn off everyone else you know, but that's ok, they're not the audience you're after.

When you focus on your audience, it also helps people who aren't part of your audience. They will know what your focus is and when they run into someone who *is* part of your audience they'll say, "I know someone you should talk to."

For example, I once saw a LinkedIn user whose headline read, "I help chiropractors in Massachusetts generate 200 new leads in their first month working with me."

Wow! That's so specific that when I met a neighbor of mine and found out his son was a chiropractor in Massachusetts, I said, "You know what, I have someone your son should talk to." Although I didn't know the guy who did lead generation for chiropractors nor did I know my neighbor's son, I was in a position to easily help both of them, all because someone on LinkedIn knew how to communicate clearly to his audience.

Talk to your audience.

Ignore everyone else.

HOMEWORK

Get clear about who your audience is and isn't.

Then talk to them—and them alone.

EXTRA CREDIT

Post this right now:

> *I'd like to refer business to you—who is your ideal customer?*

Get super-specific. Give me as much detail as you can. If you could design the perfect customer and have as many of them as you wanted, for the rest of your professional life, what would that perfect customer be like?

For example, my ideal customer is . . . [include demographics, professional details, etc.].

What about you? Tell me in the comments.

SECTION 2

OPTIMIZE YOUR PROFILE

My coauthor, Virginie Cantin, specializes in optimizing LinkedIn profiles. In her experience, the most effective profiles have two things in common.

First, if you want to truly master LinkedIn, you need to optimize for the algorithm. This will help you rank better in LinkedIn search results so that the right people will find you quickly and easily.

Second, an effective LinkedIn profile brings an individual's personal brand to life. If your profile has a human touch, it will be easier for people who visit your profile to connect and resonate with you or your business. It will be easier for them to visualize themselves working with you.

I would add that a great LinkedIn profile establishes the competency and credibility of its owner. The people you work with want to know if you will get the job done.

In this section, you'll learn how to make the changes to your profile that will get LinkedIn's algorithm working for you, provide a human touch, and establish yourself as a credible and competent leader, partner, or employee.

Ready to begin making changes to your profile? In this section you'll be making a *lot* of changes (a little each day), so get excited—your profile is in for an extreme makeover!

DAY 6

WRITE YOUR BIO OR "ABOUT" IN THE FIRST PERSON

Sandra Long, author of *LinkedIn for Personal Branding: The Ultimate Guide*, recommends using first-person language consistently throughout your entire profile in order to create a better, more human connection.

First person is when you say "I did this."

Third person is when you say "Tom did this," which sometimes people do on LinkedIn, referring to themselves.

Writing in the first person is personal, friendly, and warm. Writing in the third person is formal, stiff, professional, cold, and distant. It makes your LinkedIn page sound like a Wikipedia entry.

I understand why people write their bio in the third person—it sounds more professional, or at least that's the idea. There's a time and place for the third person, such as when you are speaking at a conference and the event organizer needs your bio for their website, but on LinkedIn, a bio written in the third person comes across as aloof, out of touch, and stuffy.

I've performed multiple surveys asking LinkedIn users what the #1 thing they want from LinkedIn is. Invariably, the top answer is "meaningful relationships." If that's also what you want, then create the content for your profile as though you were speaking to an old friend in a cafe, or in other words, use the first person. This will humanize you and make it easier for you to create a warm connection.

HOMEWORK

Scour your profile to find any instances where you've described yourself in the third person and switch it to first person.

EXTRA CREDIT

You know the drill. Post this:

> *I've written the About section on my profile in the first-person so that it comes across as more personable. At the same time, I want it to be professional. Would you take a look and let me know what you think, and if you have any suggestions for improvement I'd love to hear them!*

Note: LinkedIn posts don't need to be long to be effective. Even a short and simple post will get people talking.

DAY 7

USE A PHOTO THAT HELPS PEOPLE RECOGNIZE YOU IN REAL LIFE

LinkedIn says profiles with photos get twenty-one times more views and nine times more connection requests. However, don't use just *any* photo on LinkedIn—you should use one that is both professional and recognizable.

Your photo shows up EVERYWHERE you are on LinkedIn, from the connection requests you send to others, to the comments you make on posts, to your profile page (you know, the place where employers go to see if they want to hire you, and partners and employees go to see if they want to work with you).

Good news: a great LinkedIn photo is easy to create. First, make sure you're facing natural light, like a window (never take a photo with a window behind you), but avoid bright light that creates harsh shadows. Beware of "active" backgrounds like trees or plants (a solid background is better), and dress appropriately. Take out your phone, point it at yourself, snap a selfie, crop it square (at least 400 by 400 px), perhaps apply a subtle filter, and you're good to go—for now.

So easy, yet . . . many people make mistakes, like using a photo:

- that is thuggish (a guy flexing his muscles—and he's not a personal trainer or bodybuilder)
- that is overly serious
- that isn't serious enough (LinkedIn is not the place to show what a party-animal you are)
- where they're lost in a group of colleagues
- where they're dressed in wedding clothes . . . because it's their wedding photo
- where they're hunting in the woods—in full camouflage

I've seen all these examples—and more, and let's not even talk about profile photos that are poorly cropped, or too small, or that are low-resolution and pixelated, or that have been distorted and squeezed out of proportion.

Your photo should be professional *and* allow us to recognize you in real life. If you feel like your selfie attempts aren't cutting it, or if you want something better than what you can take with your phone, it's time to hire a professional.

Whether you take the photo yourself or hire a professional, ask whether someone will see you as credible and competent, given the image you use on your profile. Then, ask yourself, "Will the person I meet in a crowded coffee shop know who I am just by seeing my profile photo?"

Also, your LinkedIn profile photo isn't just a photo anymore. In addition to your photo, you can record a "cover story," or up to thirty seconds of video to introduce yourself. To add this video, you have to use the LinkedIn app. You can use your phone to create the video, or upload an existing video from your phone. Bonus! Once you record your video, visitors to your profile will see an orange ring around your profile photo and the video will display automatically for three seconds (with the sound off)—your profile visitor can then opt to turn the sound on and watch the full video. This is a great opportunity to make your profile more interactive and help people get a better feel for who you are in real life.

HOMEWORK

1. If your LinkedIn profile photo isn't as good as you'd like it to be, get a new one. Have a friend take it on your phone, go find a local photography studio that takes headshots for a reasonable price, or search on Instagram with the hashtag #linkedinheadshot and find a local professional photographer who knows how to do it right.

2. If you don't already have it, download the LinkedIn app. Add a short video to your photo.

EXTRA CREDIT

Post this:

> *If someone you knew only through LinkedIn met you in real life, would they be able to recognize you from your LinkedIn photo?*
>
> *What makes a great LinkedIn photo, in your opinion? I'd like to know—leave your comments below.*
>
> *Also, have you taken advantage of the feature that allows you to record 30 seconds of video that plays in the place of your LinkedIn profile photo? If so, let me know, I'd love to take a look at what you did there.*

Put that message on LinkedIn and you'll get valuable feedback. You'll also find out who your real friends are :-).

DAY 8

CUSTOMIZE YOUR URL

This task is not mission-critical, but it's super easy and takes all of a few seconds. It also may make a difference in how others perceive you because a customized LinkedIn URL looks more professional—so why not do it right now?

To change your public profile URL:

1. Click the "Me" icon at the top of your LinkedIn homepage.
2. Click "View profile."
3. On your profile page, click "Edit public profile & URL" on the right rail.
4. Under "Edit URL" in the right rail, click the "Edit" icon next to your public profile URL (it'll be an address that looks like www.linkedin.com/in/yourname).
5. Type the last part of your new custom URL in the text box (with no spaces).
6. Click "Save."

I recommend you make your URL your name. Mine is linkedin.com/in/joshuasteimle.

If your name is already taken, add a hyphen, try your last name first, or create another variation. Don't use numbers, since that makes it look like it hasn't been customized or that you were beaten to the punch by someone else (e.g., avoid something like linkedin.com/in/joshuasteimle0123).

Warning: Bear in mind that if you customize your URL, your old URL will die instantly. It will NOT redirect to your new URL. So if you've linked to your current URL from five hundred places and it would be a royal pain to try and update them all, then it isn't worth changing.

This is the exact situation I'm in. I would prefer to change my URL to /joshsteimle instead of /joshuasteimle, since professionally I always use "Josh" instead of "Joshua," but I can't because I've been on too many podcasts and in too many articles that have linked to my LinkedIn profile—and I don't want all those links to go to a "Not Found" page on LinkedIn's site. If you're just starting to grow your presence on LinkedIn, now is the time to change your URL so you don't end up stuck like me.

HOMEWORK

Update your URL to be your name, and only your name (no numbers).

EXTRA CREDIT

Post this:

> *I changed my LinkedIn URL to . . . [put your new URL here].*
>
> *If you're curious how to update your own URL to get rid of the numbers and junk LinkedIn puts on the end, here's how:*
>
> 1. *Click the "Me" icon at the top of your LinkedIn homepage.*
> 2. *Click "View profile."*

3. *On your profile page, click "Edit public profile & URL" on the right rail.*

4. *Under "Edit URL" in the right rail, click the "Edit" icon next to your public profile URL (it'll be an address that looks like www.linkedin.com/in/yourname).*

5. *Type the last part of your new custom URL in the text box.*

6. *Click "Save."*

Your connections will appreciate you passing this easy tip along.

DAY 9

MAKE FULL USE OF YOUR BANNER

Your banner is that big horizontal image behind your profile photo. If you haven't uploaded anything, you'll see a default grey design.

You may have thought about using that space before, and then thought, "Bah, I'm not a designer—and who cares what I put there? If I put up a photo of a landscape or a fish or something, what difference will it make?"

None.

That is, putting a photo of a landscape or a fish or something artsy, but meaningless, will not make a difference.

It also won't make a difference if you put those types of images up on a billboard, and yet people pay thousands of dollars each month to rent billboard space.

Start thinking like a billboard advertiser and ask yourself what you would do if you had a free $5,000/month billboard spot—because that's what LinkedIn is giving you. Are you wasting that space by using LinkedIn's default grey graphic? Time to put that real estate to productive use.

String Nguyen uses her banner to reinforce her personal brand as a LinkedIn content expert.

Alexandra Galviz lists her value proposition and displays client logos to communicate authority and credibility.

Richard Moore displays his personal brand tagline in his banner that says, "I help consultants get clients on LinkedIn using sales and content," and invites those who are interested to "Message me to learn more."

I can't tell you exactly what to put in *your* banner space on your LinkedIn profile—it depends on what your purpose is on LinkedIn—but whatever you choose, it should:

1. Reinforce your personal brand.
2. Make you look more impressive than if you left the default grey.
3. Be easy to understand. If a casual visitor has to spend more than two or three seconds processing it, it's too complicated.

HOMEWORK

Put your banner space to use by using it to reinforce who you are, what you do, and who you do it for.

EXTRA CREDIT

Once you've created a new banner, post this:

> *I put up a new banner on my LinkedIn profile. I chose an image that . . .* [explain what it is and why you chose it].
>
> *My goals are to help people understand who I am, what I do, and who I do it for, making my profile look better.*

What's one thing I could do to improve it? Would love your feedback.

Thanks!

DAY 10

USE YOUR EXPERIENCE SECTION TO GET REAL

Many people on LinkedIn treat the Experience section as a resume. They list bullet points of duties and tasks they were given, achievements they accomplished, and so on.

There's nothing *wrong* with that, except that it's boring, not to mention it's the same thing everyone else is doing.

Stand out by adding stories to each of your work experiences. Tell us:

- What you were hired to do
- What challenges you faced doing it
- How you overcame those challenges to achieve success
- What you learned in the process

Write this as though you were meeting with a close friend for lunch—someone who would be excited to hear about it, but who knows you well enough that you don't need to impress them.

By getting human and letting everyone on LinkedIn take a peek at what it's like to be you, you'll make your profile visitors feel like they already know you. Your vulnerability will encourage them to trust you. By showing them how you overcame your challenges, they'll trust you to help them overcome *their* challenges. That's especially valuable when the person viewing your profile is someone who wants to hire you or your business.

HOMEWORK

For your current work experience, tell a story about:

- What you were hired to do (or if you run your own business, why you started it)
- What challenges you faced doing it
- How you overcame those challenges to achieve success
- The concrete achievements you've made
- What you learned in the process

Then move on to your next work experience, and so on.

If you have extensive work experience, do this for at least your most recent three positions, plus any others that are particularly relevant to what you're doing today or want to do in the future.

Note: Adam Houlahan, author of *The LinkedIn Playbook*, only lists his work experience that is directly related to his primary focus right now—attracting clients to his LinkedIn agency. While I prefer to show more of my work history, whether or not it's directly relevant to my current focus, Adam's approach is also perfectly valid.

EXTRA CREDIT

Post this:

> *What's the best job you've ever had, other than your current one?*

> *For me, it was . . . [talk about your favorite prior job and include details about what you were hired to do, the challenges, how you overcame the challenges, what you achieved, and what you learned].*
>
> *What has been a favorite job of yours, and why?*

Writing this post may help you think of additional ways to improve your experience section. If it does, go make those edits!

DAY 11

MAKE YOUR HEADLINE SAY WHAT MATTERS MOST

Your headline is the line of bold text next to your photo where most people simply put their job title (some people refer to your LinkedIn headline as your "LinkedIn title"). Felipe Lodi from WorkFlow ICT Ireland says, "Your headline is the most valuable real estate in your profile, because it plays for your benefit even when you are not connected to people." However, despite how important the headline is, many people use their job title and nothing else as their headline on LinkedIn and this is a problem because it doesn't tell anyone what they *do.*

CEO, CMO, VP Sales, Director HR, Product Marketer, Frontline Systems Engineer Level 3 . . .

Unless you have an obviously high-ranking title at a well-known company, like "CEO of Facebook" or "CMO at GE," these titles are almost meaningless. The other exception is if your title makes it obvious what you do, like "Staff Writer at Mashable."

However, if you're not Mark Zuckerberg, instead of merely listing your title, tell us what you do, who you do it for, and the results you deliver.

For example:

- I help new entrepreneurs generate sales through Facebook ads
- I build HR strategies for Western companies doing business in China
- I teach marketing agency CEOs how to go from $3M to $10M

If you were at a networking event and someone asked what you do, you'd have a chance to explain, but on LinkedIn, many people won't look past your headline unless it hooks them, and you've got only a few seconds for that to happen. In his book *Hook Point: How To Stand Out In A 3-Second World*, author Brendan Kane says, "If you can't capture people's attention in those first three seconds . . . then you can't get them to pay attention to the rest of your story, products, or services."[6]

If your headline says what you do, and it matches the needs of the person looking at your profile, you've made it much more likely they'll read the rest of your LinkedIn profile and contact you.

You also significantly increase the likelihood of being referred to relevant opportunities by your connections. When your headline clearly states what you do and who you do it for, you'll be top of mind for them when a match comes along.

"If you want to know how to write a great headline, look at how copywriters write theirs," says my coauthor Aaron Wrixon, a copywriter and content strategist who writes and edits hundreds of thousands of his and others' words every year. Copywriters know how

---

[6] Brendan Kane. *Hook Point: How To Stand Out In A 3-second World.* 2020. Introduction, p. xx.

to create a click-worthy headline (which is really what your LinkedIn headline is).

One way to do that? Use author, entrepreneur, and legendary copywriter Michael Masterson's 4U Formula[7]:

- Urgent: What makes someone want to act—in this case, find out about you—now, instead of tomorrow or never at all?
- Unique: What makes you different?
- Useful: What's in it for them?
- Ultra-specific: What are your audience's pain points? How does what you do make their lives better?

In addition to using the 4U Formula, Aaron recommends "front-loading" the first forty characters of your headline. This will communicate the valuable benefits you offer even if the headline gets cut off in LinkedIn's mobile version of its Messaging app.

For example, Aaron's headline reads "I make marketing better. Content writer & strategist for agencies & their clients. Coauthor, Get Rich in the Deep End." His first forty characters? "I make marketing better. Content writer"—which tells you everything you need to know if you're curious about working with a writer.

HOMEWORK

Modify your headline to start with what you do and who you do it for. Be specific. If you must use your official job title, tack it onto the end. If you have the space, include keywords. These will help you show up in relevant search results.

---

[7] See https://smallbusiness.yahoo.com/advisor/resource-center/4-u-copywriting-tips-writing-great-headlines-copy-220008437. Accessed 28 September 2021.

EXTRA CREDIT

Post this:

> *What's one thing I could do to improve my new LinkedIn headline/title?*
>
> *I just updated it to explain what I do and who I do it for, as well as the results I deliver, but I'd like to make it even better. Is there anything missing? Confusing? All suggestions are welcome.*
>
> *Thanks!*

DAY 12

YOUR ABOUT SECTION—MAKE THE FIRST THREE LINES COUNT

When writing your bio or summary—officially known as the "About" section—on LinkedIn, make the first three lines count.

Why? Because that's all people see at first until they expand the section. (This applies to both mobile and desktop.)

In other words, if you don't hook your reader in the first three lines of your bio, they're not going to read the rest. The rest of your bio may be amazing, but they'll never know.

"In my opinion, the best LinkedIn summaries tell a story," says Lacey Abbacchi. "The goal is to be personable and go beyond just sharing your accomplishments, accolades, and professional experience. Now, that's not to say that those aspects aren't important; believe me, they are. However, people are much more likely to hear what you have to say if they feel like they know you."[8]

What should you put in those first three lines?

---

[8] Personal communication with Josh Steimle.

It depends who you are, but consider answering these questions when writing your opener:

- What is your goal?
- What is your genius zone, the combination of knowledge, experience, skills, and traits that make you unique? (See Day 4)
- Who is your ideal audience?
- What content (i.e., words, phrases, ideas) will trigger their interest and get them to expand your summary to read the rest of it?

Nathan Hirsch, CEO of the virtual assistant marketplace Freeeup, says, "Think of the first sentence or two of your LinkedIn bio as your personal elevator pitch. What do you want them to know within the first ten seconds? Who are you? Who do you help? How do you add value to the world?"

Sandra Long coaches her clients to think of the About section as more of an introduction. "Try to create immediate interest with a personal story of how you help your clients."

"Great About section intros start with the repetition of the headline," my coauthor Virginie Cantin says. "Then, make sure you check the most important boxes, the ones that matter to your ideal audience so that they'll want to keep reading."

Here are examples of great "About" intros.

"I help entrepreneurs build businesses online. My areas of expertise include how to start and grow an email list, how to create digital courses and how to promote and sell courses online using webinars."

— Amy Porterfield

Here, Amy lets us know exactly who she works with and what her service is. If you're an entrepreneur trying to build an email list, is there any way you could resist reading the rest of her bio?

"I'm a leadership mentor. Together with my team at Michael Hyatt & Co., I help overwhelmed high achievers win at work, succeed at life, and lead with confidence."

— Michael Hyatt

The key word in Michael's intro to his About section is "overwhelmed." Similar to Amy, Michael knows who his audience is and speaks directly to them.

"Experienced author, editor, ghostwriter of 10+ books and creative coach. I've helped hundreds of writers, from total beginners to New York Times Bestsellers to write, edit and publish their projects and discover the power writing can have to improve your sleep, increase your confidence, strengthen your relationships, keep you from getting sick and . . ."

— Allison Fallon

If I were looking for a ghostwriter to help me write a book, Allison's intro would catch my eye.

You may notice that Allison's bio cuts off in the middle of a sentence, which is fine—perhaps even preferable. There's something about it getting cut off that almost makes it more tantalizing to click. . . . (Don't *you* want to finish reading that sentence?)

HOMEWORK

Rewrite the first three or four lines of your bio or "About" section. Use storytelling. Focus on what you do, who you do it for, and the results you deliver to create a hook. That way, when your ideal audience reads it, they'll be compelled to read the rest.

EXTRA CREDIT

Post this after you take a stab at rewriting those first lines:

> *I recently learned that the first three lines of your bio on your LinkedIn profile are the most important because if people don't like what they read there, they won't click "See more" to see the rest.*
>
> *I rewrote the first three lines of my bio to say:*
>
> *[Include the first three lines of your bio here]*
>
> *Does this make you want to read more? What's one thing I could do to improve it and make it more compelling?*
>
> *I would love any feedback you have to offer as I'm working on improving my profile to better focus on my ideal audience and tell them who I am, what I do, and who I do it for.*
>
> *Thanks!*

EXTRA EXTRA CREDIT

If you really want to take your profile to the next level, consider structuring and crafting your "About" section like a sales letter.

Why? Because it acts like a landing page. Someone either searches for your profile or reads your content and clicks through. You've got their attention. Now's your opportunity to maximize your chances of winning their business rather than leaving it to chance.

To do so, answer the following questions in sequence:

Who are you targeting? What are they struggling with? What have they tried before that has failed? Why is your solution different and effective? What results have you achieved for similar clients? Who have you worked with that might lend you credibility? What's the call to action for them to take (this might be a link to your Calendly or even a simple "message me")?

DAY 13

TELL US HOW TO SAY YOUR NAME

How would you say my last name?

S - T - E - I - M - L - E

Unless you're a native German speaker, you're probably saying it wrong (I'm in my forties, and I can count on one hand the number of people who have pronounced it correctly on the first try).

To help difficult-last-name folks like me, and especially to facilitate correct name pronunciation across different languages where even simple or common names may be mispronounced, LinkedIn rolled out a feature that allows you to record yourself saying your name.

To record your name, you must use the LinkedIn app, not the desktop site.

Within the app, edit your profile and under "Name pronunciation" add a recording. LinkedIn gives you ten seconds to record, which was enough for me to say, "Steimle . . . rhymes with timely" on my recording.

HOMEWORK

Use the mobile app to record your name.

Remember, even if your name is John Smith and you think, "Oh c'mon, everyone knows how to say my name," that may not be the case with people whose native language isn't English.

EXTRA CREDIT

Try this post out:

> *"A person's name is to that person, the sweetest, most important sound in any language." — Dale Carnegie*
>
> *How do you remember the names of your customers, clients, and other people you work with?*
>
> *Do you use a memory trick?*
>
> *[share your own if you've got one]*
>
> *I'd love to hear how you do it in the comments below.*

DAY 14

ADD HONORS, AWARDS, AND OTHER PROOF

Note: If you don't already have this section visible on your profile, then to add it click on "Add Section" in the upper right while editing your profile, then select the appropriate option under "Accomplishments."

Many people feel uncomfortable adding honors and awards to their LinkedIn profiles. It feels a bit "icky," like you're giving yourself a trophy.

I get it. It feels awkward. But reverse the roles and think about people you know and their profiles. If you went to their profile and saw "E&Y Entrepreneur of the Year" listed under honors and awards would you think, "Show off, give me a break," or would you say, "Wow! That's great!"

I'd like to believe most of us want to be cheerleaders for each other and encourage one another to greatness. When someone adds an award or honor to their profile, it allows the rest of us to celebrate them.

In addition, listing your official accomplishments and the recognition you've received may make the difference between getting the attention you want, whether from an employer, partner, or client. If you were the top sales rep at your company last year, don't you think a prospective employer would like to know that?

If you're not sure what to list, here are some ideas:

- Have you been recognized for a professional achievement?
- Have you ever been quoted in the media, such as a newspaper or magazine?
- Do you sit on any boards or special committees?
- Do you have any plaques, certificates, or trophies?

Any recognition that is relevant to your professional focus is fair game.

Still stuck? My coauthor Aaron Wrixon suggests five different kinds of proof that show other people you're the real deal:

- **Expertise.** What kind of experience do you have? How many years have you been in business? How many projects have you completed? How many clients have you helped?
- **Credentials.** What degrees or certifications do you have? What—you guessed it—honors or awards have you won?
- **References.** What case studies or customer experiences can you talk about? What reviews or recommendations from others can you share?
- **Numbers.** What money or time have you made or saved for others? What measures have you increased or decreased?
- **Altruism.** What good have you done in the world? How have you helped others?

Bear in mind, when you're adding *any* honors, awards, or proof, you should avoid listing irrelevant or outdated things that make you look small and desperate instead of accomplished and confident. (That participation trophy from your t-ball team when you were five years old? Probably better to keep that to yourself.)

HOMEWORK

Add relevant honors, awards, and other proof to your profile.

EXTRA CREDIT

This one may require a bit more thought than some of the other posts, because I'm asking you to dig into your memories and find a story about when someone praised you, and it really meant something. If it's hard to find an experience that matches this post, customize it to make it work:

> *What's the best praise, honor, or award you've ever received?*
>
> *For me, it wasn't sports trophies I got as a kid, professional certifications, or any sort of official recognition, it was just two words.*
>
> *I was working hard on a project, and my boss came by to check in. He looked at the work I was doing and simply said, "Good job." I knew he understood the work I was doing and I knew he was sincere—it wasn't empty praise. Two little words, but they meant a lot to me.*
>
> *What recognition at work has meant the most to you?*

This really happened to me, but I bet it's a story many others could tell. If you have a similar story, post it. If you can change it to make it your own, post that. Instead of a boss, perhaps it was a parent or teacher. Maybe they didn't say, "Good job," but used other words. Whatever the case, post about when you received praise that meant a lot to you.

DAY 15

DON'T TELL—SHOW

"I have a popular podcast."

Too many people on LinkedIn use phrases like this to describe their accomplishments, and my coauthor Virginie Cantin says this is the #1 mistake her clients make.

Instead of telling your audience how awesome you are, SHOW them!

Lewis Howes does this the right way in his LinkedIn bio. Howes has a great podcast—and yes, it's quite popular, but listen to how he proves it, without ever needing to use those words:

> *The School of Greatness podcast reaches 3 million people monthly and frequents the top 10 on iTunes each month.*

Boom!

(Free bonus tip: Don't ever say "Boom!" like I just did—on LinkedIn or off.)

When you give readers the facts, they take care of the self-promotion, without you needing to point out your greatness.

Of course, if the facts aren't that impressive, then you'd be tempted to tell, rather than show, right? That's the point. If you're telling instead of showing, you look as though the facts aren't on your side—so this doesn't do you any good, no matter what.

There's only one way to win this game, and that's to build something worth showing off.

If your podcast only gets five downloads per month, get it to fifty, then five hundred, then five thousand, then fifty thousand.

If your newsletter only has five subscribers, then work to get it to one hundred thousand.

Until then, you don't have anything to show off, so focus your attention on serving others and building something great. Your audience is looking forward to seeing what you've accomplished.

HOMEWORK

Check your profile to get rid of fluff. Replace it with concrete achievements.

EXTRA CREDIT

Post this:

> *What's a number in your professional life you're proud of?*
>
> *It could be a sales target you hit, people you've influenced, talks you've given, days you brought your kids to work, or anything else.*
>
> *For me, it's . . . [tell your number and your story].*
>
> *What's your number?*

DAY 16

VOLUNTEER—AND LIST IT

Note: If this section isn't already showing on your LinkedIn profile, go to "Add Section," then "Background," then "Volunteer experience."

Imagine you're an employer, and you're looking at the LinkedIn profiles of two candidates. They both look excellent. However, one lists her volunteer experience and details about what she did, how she felt about it, and what she accomplished. The other has nothing in his Volunteer experience section.

Which candidate would you feel you knew better?

Who would you feel has a more diverse background?

Who would you feel is more of a self-starter and motivated to do a great job working with you?

Which one would you feel is more altruistic and likely to do a better job?

Let's take things a step further.

Let's imagine the profile with volunteer experiences says that she used to be on the board of a community organization that supports adoption—and you happen to have adopted a child. Now which candidate are you (EVEN MORE) interested in talking to?

Your volunteer section is an opportunity for you to show that you're well-rounded—and maybe even make an emotional connection with a prospective employer, partner, or customer.

While it may be awkward to list what you've done as a volunteer, as though you're showing off your charitable nature, that's not how it comes across to most people reading your profile. It's helpful information that is interesting and provides more depth. So go ahead, list it, and include details about what you did, the challenges you faced, how you overcame them, and how the experience has made you a better person.

Bonus insight from my coauthor Virginie Cantin:

While job descriptions in your experience section get truncated after a few lines, this isn't the case in the volunteer section. You have up to two thousand characters to describe your volunteer experience, and if you do, LinkedIn will show it all. This alone indicates how valuable volunteering is on LinkedIn.

What if you don't have any volunteer experience to list?

Go get some. It could change your life and the lives of many others.

HOMEWORK

If you have volunteer experience that's not listed on your LinkedIn profile, add it. Give us lots of detail.

If you don't have volunteer experience to list, find a cause you believe in and help out. If you're not sure where to start, check out JustServe.org.

EXTRA CREDIT

Post this:

How have volunteer experiences benefitted you professionally?

Short. Sweet. Easy. Done.

Feel free to answer the question yourself as part of the post.

DAY 17

PICK THE "OTHER" WEBSITE OPTION

This is one of those minor details about your LinkedIn profile that isn't critical at all but is a fun little trick.

You have the option to add up to three website URLs to your profile by clicking on "Contact info" (just below your photo, name, and headline), then clicking on the pencil, then "Add website."

I chose to include websites for each of my two companies, plus my personal brand/blog website.

The drop-down menu gives you the option to label these websites as:

- Company
- Personal
- Blog
- RSS feed
- Portfolio
- Other

If you choose "Company" or "Personal" then when people view your contact information it will show a link labeled "Company" that links to your company website, or "Personal" that links to your personal website.

Fair enough, but if you choose "Other" then it gives you the option to label the link however you want.

If I want to say "MWI" for my first company website, I can say MWI, or I can say "My Marketing Agency Website" or whatever I want, up to thirty characters! Isn't that better than saying "Company" or something generic?

HOMEWORK

1. Add URLs to your LinkedIn profile if you haven't already.
2. Label them using the "Other" option.

EXTRA CREDIT

Post this:

> *Do you have a personal brand website? Do you think it's a valuable tool?*
>
> *If you look at people's contact info on their LinkedIn profile, some have links to their personal website that has more information about them as a consultant, speaker, author, etc.*
>
> *Do you think a personal brand website is a valuable tool, the type of thing everyone needs, or is it just for some people?*

For the record, I have a personal brand website (JoshSteimle.com) and it's been valuable for me. I believe almost everyone could benefit from one, but that's different than saying everyone needs one. Since it takes time and money to build and maintain one, everyone needs to do a cost-benefit analysis to see if it makes sense for them. By creating the post above, you'll find out which of your contacts have personal brand websites and you'll be able to see what they're doing with them.

DAY 18

ADD DETAILS TO YOUR EDUCATION SECTION

I know you.

We may have never met and I might not know your name, but I know you.

Right now, I bet if I visit your LinkedIn profile and look at your education section, I'll see a list of schools, perhaps the years you attended them, the degree you earned, and that's it. No other details.

Am I right?

(See? I told you I know you.)

LinkedIn recently allowed us to add much more information to our education section. But don't worry—you're not behind everyone else, because nobody else has updated their education section either.

The good news is, now you can get ahead. Consider adding:

1. **Your story.** Tell us why you chose your school and your program. Tell us how you struggled to get in, how you struggled to get through, and how you worked to overcome your challenges. Tell us what this school and the degree you earned have meant to you.

2. **Media.** Add links, not only to websites, but to videos, presentations, and documents. If you've published papers or accomplished something, link to it here.

3. **Lessons learned.** What would you do differently if you could go back? What advice do you have for students who are currently in your program?

There's so much more you can add here to show visitors to your profile that you're a real, authentic human being with an exciting backstory.

In this section, you have up to a thousand characters for each description. As in the volunteer section, LinkedIn doesn't truncate anything.

HOMEWORK

Make sure your education information is up to date.

Add details for each educational experience including your story and media items.

EXTRA CREDIT

Post this:

> *What's one thing you learned in school, at any age, that is useful to you professionally today?*
>
> *One of the most valuable things I learned in school was . . . [tell your story].*
>
> *What about you?*

DAY 19

FEATURE YOURSELF

The employer who wants to hire you, the partner who wants to work with you, and the employee who wants to work for you, all want the same thing. They want to know who you are, and they want to get to know you in the way they feel most comfortable consuming information.

Some people like to read text.

Others prefer to watch a video, look at a slide deck, or view an image.

Just as each member of your audience prefers a different format for content, you may prefer to create one type of media rather than another. For example, I'm much more comfortable writing what I think vs. making a video about it. Happily, LinkedIn allows you to communicate with your audience in many different ways, including through the Featured section of your profile.

To better showcase my work as a writer, I've used my Featured section to post my articles on *Forbes*, *Mashable*, *Fortune*, and other publications. I've linked to slide decks, PDFs, videos, and my blog posts as well. You can also feature your LinkedIn posts. (My coauthor Aaron Wrixon has even featured video testimonials from happy clients.)

Pro tip: Include a title that shows up when you display it in the Featured section. For example, I include a photo at the top of all my blog posts and I put the blog post title on that graphic in large white letters while darkening the photo behind it to increase the contrast. When I link to my blog posts in the Featured section of my profile, it pulls in that photo with the title on it, making it easy for people to know what they'll get if they click through.

If you only include a photo on your blog post, perhaps because the title is displayed on your blog as HTML text above the photo, then LinkedIn will pull in the photo which is going to take up a lot of space but won't necessarily be helpful for your profile visitors. The same goes for videos—make sure the title shows up on the graphic that LinkedIn automatically pulls in.

HOMEWORK

Look for quick, easy wins like links to blog posts, videos, presentations, and other content you already have published elsewhere, and post these in your Featured section.

EXTRA CREDIT

Post this:

> *What kind of content do you like the best on LinkedIn? What catches your eye?*
>
> *Do you prefer reading text posts?*
>
> *Do you like watching videos?*
>
> *Do you listen to podcasts people post to LinkedIn?*
>
> *Do you read blog posts when people link to them?*

What do you like, and what do you wish there were more of? What do you wish there were less of?

Looking forward to your responses!

DAY 20

ADD LANGUAGES

Even if you don't speak more than one language, you can create multiple language versions of your profile to attract international attention.

It used to be that if you spoke more than one language, you could list them on your profile and it would show "I speak English, Spanish, and Mandarin Chinese." Now, you can do much more. To quote LinkedIn:

> *You can create your profile in a language that is different from your default profile. While you can't change the language of your primary profile, you can create as many additional language profiles from the options available.*[9]

And LinkedIn gives us the reason why we might want to do this:

"Having multiple language profiles makes it easier for other members and recruiters to find you."

---

[9] "LinkedIn Help: Create or Delete a Profile in Another Language." Accessed 16 September 2021. https://www.linkedin.com/help/linkedin/answer/1717/create-or-delete-a-profile-in-another-language.

For example, imagine that Marcela, an intern for a major association based in Colombia, has been asked to find a speaker on digital transformation to speak at the association's international event. The event will be held in Colombia, but will be in English, not Spanish, to appeal to the global audience. However, Marcela does not speak or read English beyond a basic level.

As Marcela begins her search on LinkedIn for a suitable speaker for this event, she naturally gravitates towards reading profiles that are in Spanish, her native language. She hopes to come across one who shows that they also speak English fluently enough to be hired to speak at this event.

If you're a great fit to speak at this event, but you only have a profile in English, chances are, Marcela will never find your profile.

But what if you created a secondary language profile in Spanish? Then you'd be more likely to come up in Marcela's search. You can state that you only present in English, but have a Spanish profile because you're happy to travel.

Win-win, muchacho.

I have my profile in multiple languages; English, Portuguese, and simplified and traditional Chinese. That's because I'm a native English speaker, I'm fluent in Portuguese, and can get by in China. I should add Spanish, since I can get along in Spanish even better than I can in Chinese.

(If you're curious, I learned some Spanish in high school. I learned Portuguese while serving as a missionary for The Church of Jesus Christ of Latter-day Saints in Manaus, Brazil. And I learned some Cantonese and a bit of Mandarin Chinese living in Hong Kong and Shenzhen from 2013 to 2018.)

To create your profile in another language:

1. Click the "Me" icon at the top of your LinkedIn homepage.
2. Click "View profile."
3. Click "Add profile in another language" on the right rail.
4. Choose a language from the dropdown list and update your first and last name if they're different in the new profile's language. If the language you want to add isn't listed in the dropdown, your current profile may already be in that language. Make sure your profile's content is in the same language as the language profile you've selected.
5. Translate your existing headline. (Translations aren't done for you. You'll need to supply the content in your language of choice.)
6. Click "Create Profile."

HOMEWORK

If you want to find opportunities where other languages are spoken, add versions of your profile in those languages.

EXTRA CREDIT

Post this:

> *What languages do you speak and where did you learn?*
>
> *Just curious to know more about my network.*

If you speak more than one language or have language interests, talk about that in your post.

DAY 21

MAKE IT EASY TO CONTACT YOU

I include my email address in my LinkedIn About section. Does that mean it gets harvested by spammers?

Probably.

Do I care?

No.

My email provider offers great spam filtering and whatever inconvenience is left over adds up to a few minutes each month. If that's the price I pay to make it easier for potential clients to contact me, it's well worth it.

Other ways to make it easy to contact you:

- Make sure the email in your LinkedIn account is accurate, so messages sent to you through LinkedIn don't go into a black hole. Edit this by going to Settings & Privacy, clicking on "Sign in & security."
- Configure your notification settings to email you whenever someone reaches out. Do this by going to Settings & Privacy, clicking on "Communications," then clicking on "How you get

your notifications." Alternatively, make it part of your daily routine to check your LinkedIn messages.

- In the About section, include your phone number if that's your preferred mode of communication.

Nathan Hirsch says, "You can even go as far as sharing your calendar link in your profile. I openly share my Calendly and regularly meet amazing people because of that openness. You'll be surprised how far being available will take you with others."[10]

The easier you make it for people to contact you, the more likely they will do so.

HOMEWORK

Check your contact information as outlined above to make sure it's up to date.

Add contact information to your About section.

EXTRA CREDIT

Post this:

> *What's your preferred way to have the first conversation with someone you don't know?*
>
> *In person, phone, email, texting?*
>
> *For me, I prefer . . . [specify your preferred method].*
>
> *What about you?*

---

[10] Personal communication with Josh Steimle.

DAY 22

USE KEYWORDS

Question: If you're searching for a new job, would you rather have five prospective employers look at your LinkedIn profile, or five hundred?

It's a trick question, because the correct answer is that you'd rather have five of the right people visit your profile than five hundred of the wrong people. Of course, you'd rather have five hundred of the right kind vs. five of any kind.

The real trick is to use keywords strategically on your LinkedIn profile in order to show up more often in LinkedIn's search for terms related to what you want to. That will attract the right attention from lots of the right people.

If you've ever done a little SEO (search engine optimization) on your website so that it will show up higher in searches on Google, you already know how this works. LinkedIn contains a search engine that works like Google, but whereas Google searches anything and everything that's online, LinkedIn only searches itself. Knowing how LinkedIn's search works is your ticket to increased attention.

For example, if you want a programming job, having the word "programming" somewhere on your profile would make sense, but this won't be enough. What kind of programming do you want to do? How specific can you get?

This is where many people get it wrong on LinkedIn. They think by using lots of more generic keywords, they'll come up in lots of searches. Maybe they will (if they're lucky), but they'll be attracting lots of the wrong people.

The more specific you are about what you want to do, the more you'll attract the right kind of people. In addition, if you use highly specific keywords, your audience will get more excited when they find you because you'll appear to be a perfect match.

When choosing keywords, think about search intent, or what the person whose attention you want is trying to do. Think about what keywords they will search for and why. Think about where to place those keywords so they will see them quickly. Even if LinkedIn changes in the future (it will), by learning to think about search intent, you'll always know how to use keywords appropriately.

Not all the places where you might place keywords are of equal importance. A keyword in your headline is weighted more heavily than the same keyword in your About or Experience section. Your most important keywords should go in the most prominent places (which according to Virginie Cantin are headline, current and past job titles, and skills), as well as throughout the copy on your profile.

There are many places to include keywords on your profile. If you run out of space, that's a problem I can understand, however, most people aren't using the space they've been given. They neglect to add detail to their work experience, they only use half their allotted bio space, they don't max out their fifty skills (see Day 23), etc.

How many keywords should you have? Virginie Cantin says you should have a list of ten to twenty keywords. However, you want to have up to three main keywords that you repeat in your headline and current and past job titles. Scatter the rest of your keywords throughout your About section and work experience summaries.

Here's one more important item to note—your keywords will not remain static.

My priorities change frequently, and so the keywords I use change frequently. I'm constantly tweaking my headline and bio to reflect what I'm currently working on.

Review your keyword list on a regular basis and update your profile as needed.

HOMEWORK

Make a list of keywords to use on LinkedIn. You may find it helpful to refer back to Day 4 where we learned about your genius zone.

Prioritize those keywords. Which are most important to help you get the attention you want on LinkedIn?

Scan your profile and add your keywords, in order to catch the eye of prospective employers, partners, or customers.

EXTRA CREDIT

Post this:

> *If you could only choose five keywords to tell everyone on LinkedIn who you are, what you do, and who you do it for, what would those keywords be?*
>
> *For me, they are . . . [list your keywords here].*
>
> *What are yours?*

DAY 23

ADD 50 SKILLS AND ALLOW PEOPLE TO ENDORSE YOU FOR THEM

Many people don't even know about the skills section of their LinkedIn profile. It's towards the bottom of your profile page. (If you don't see it, click on "Add Section," then click on "Skills.") In this section, you may list up to fifty skills. You can modify these skills at any time, as often as you like. People who visit your profile are invited to endorse you for those skills and LinkedIn displays how many people have endorsed you for each skill. (Up to 99, at which point it simply shows "99+.")

While you might be tempted to think these endorsements for your skills are good for your ego and little more, there's far more to it. Think about how LinkedIn might use this data. If someone types "interaction design" into the LinkedIn search bar, and you have no endorsements for that skill—but someone else has 99+ for the same skill—which person will LinkedIn show higher in the search results, all other things being equal?

But it isn't merely the number of endorsements per skill you have—the number of skills you list will also benefit you. LinkedIn says people who list at least five skills get up to seventeen times more profile views.[11] Here's how that might work:

Say, for example, you live in Boston and someone does a search for people like you in your city. Let's say you have three skills listed—but twenty thousand other people have five or more. Who's going to show up in that search and who won't?

Don't add just *any* skills though. When listing them, choose *real* skills.

Microsoft Word is not a skill you should list. Neither is something like "email." In this day and age, it's assumed everyone has these skills.

List skills someone wouldn't assume everyone already has, but be careful about choosing skills that are too generic, like "marketing." By itself, it doesn't mean anything to people searching, because nobody looks for a marketer, they're looking for a specific type of marketer or a marketer with certain skills. "Digital marketing" is more specific, but still a little generic. "Search marketing" or "social media marketing" or "performance marketing" are much more specific, therefore ideal.

If you're not sure what to put, find people like you—or who you want to be like—and see what skills they list.

What if you're getting endorsed by people for skills you don't want to be endorsed for? You can hide and delete the skills you don't want to show on your profile.

If you're not getting any endorsements on your skills, check your settings to make sure you allow people to endorse you. And, endorse others—sometimes you've got to give in order to get.

---

[11] Charu Jangid. "LinkedIn Tips to Keep Your Profile Fresh." *LinkedIn Official Blog*. Accessed 29 September 2021. https://blog.linkedin.com/2018/april/12/linkedin-tips-to-keep-your-profile-fresh.

Want to beef up the number of endorsements for a particular skill? Select it as one of the three promoted skills. At first, this might mean you're showing a low number on your profile, but it will quickly get to 99+. Once it does, switch it out so you can promote a different skill and get more endorsements on it. If you keep doing this, you'll eventually have a lot of skills with 99+ endorsements on each.

HOMEWORK

Go to your profile and scroll down to the "Skills & endorsements" section.

Click on the pencil icon on the right to edit your skills.

Add skills until you get to fifty.

Choose three skills you want to feature.

Check your settings (they're in the same area where you edit your skills). Ensure all the settings, including "I want to be endorsed" and "Include me in endorsement suggestions to my connections" are turned on. If you have any pending endorsements, click on that area and then click "Add to profile" for each pending endorsement.

EXTRA CREDIT

This is a good opportunity to call in a favor with a post like this:

> *I just finished adding skills to my LinkedIn profile. Since many of these skills are new on my profile, nobody's had a chance to endorse me for them yet. Would you mind going to my profile and endorsing me for any of the skills you know I have? I'd be happy to do the same for you.*

Of course, you better help those who help you, or LinkedIn karma will come back to bite you.

DAY 24

GET 20+ RECOMMENDATIONS

Remember when you used to give someone your resume or CV and then at the bottom you would put "References upon request"—as though any employer would *not* want to request your references? These days, your references are on your LinkedIn profile in the recommendations section, and you should have many more than the handful you would give an employer.

Get at least twenty GREAT recommendations. Twenty is the number at which someone looking at your profile says, "Wow, twenty, that's a ton of recommendations! This person must know what they're doing."

Most people have just a handful of recommendations, if they have any at all. Shoot first for five, then ten, then twenty.

Ways to get recommendations:

1. **Give recommendations.** When you give someone a recommendation, LinkedIn invites them to write one for you. Since you gave them something of value, they'll feel inclined to return the favor. Win-win.

2. **Ask for recommendations.** Each time you have a positive experience with an employer, manager, boss, coworker, or client, that's a great time to ask for a recommendation. If they

don't give you one (they may not know how), request it through LinkedIn. This will send them a message and step them through the process to make it easy.

Note: If you're playing catch up, it's understandable that you're going to reach out and make lots of requests at once. Since recommendations are date-stamped, you don't want to get a bunch all at once and then never again—you want them to be spaced out and appear organic. (Recruiters notice this type of thing.) Don't let this keep you from asking for a lot right now, but do let it motivate you to keep up with it going forward.

HOMEWORK

Give five recommendations on LinkedIn to people you know, right now.

Request one recommendation, right now.

Going through this short exercise will get you comfortable with how the process works, without overwhelming you.

Once you're finished, then proceed as appropriate to get five, then ten, and then twenty recommendations.

After you hit twenty, going forward, ask for them as the opportunity arises naturally.

EXTRA CREDIT

Post this:

> *Who is one of the best people you've ever worked with, and why?*
>
> *When I was at . . . [tell your story of a job you had and someone great you worked with].*

Tag someone you loved working with and tell me what made it a great experience for you.

Also, give that person a recommendation on LinkedIn. If you've never given a recommendation before, go to someone's profile, click on the "More" button, and then click "Recommend."

DAY 25

USE CORRECT CAPITALIZATION, SPELLING, AND GRAMMAR

On your LinkedIn profile, the first letter of each part of your name should be capitalized, like this:

Josh Steimle

This goes for all names, anywhere on your profile. As a general rule, unless you are shouting, don't use all caps anywhere on LinkedIn or it will sound like this:

JOSH STEIMLE!!!

That goes for any text, not only names—UNLESS you have a strong need to emphasize something and you use capitalization in place of italics. But this should be rare; otherwise, people will think you're an angry, shouting person.

The more common offense I see is people using all lowercase for their names, like this:

josh Steimle

This makes it look like a computer filled out your profile, which is to say, it makes your profile look fake.

Are there exceptions to the capitalization rule? Sure, but know the rule before you break it, and know why you're breaking it.

My coauthor Andy Foote capitalizes his entire name and says "My name is in all caps, but I'm not shouting, I'm announcing. As on TV, subtitles and closed captions are (usually) written in all caps for ease of reading. Also, because the vast majority of people on LinkedIn follow the first letter capitalization convention, it's easy to stand out from the crowd."

When it comes to spelling, I see so many spelling errors on profiles. I get it—we all make mistakes, but that doesn't mean it's OK. When you spell incorrectly, people assume you lack command of your language, are inattentive to detail, and may be incompetent in areas other than spelling. Poor spelling is even more inexcusable now, since even our web browsers tell us when we're misspelling words.

Of course, some words are trickier because when they're misspelled, they're still spelled "correctly." For example:

- You're vs. your
- Their vs. there
- Its vs. it's

Word and Google docs have built-in grammar checking, so they may catch these mistakes, but even they aren't 100 percent accurate, and until they are, there's no substitute for knowing how to spell correctly on your own.

Virginie Cantin says that when it comes to your keywords, you should double-check that you don't have any spelling errors in them. A keyword that is misspelled is not a keyword. In other words, the algorithm won't autocorrect your mistake when crawling your profile, so you won't rank for the keywords you misspell.

With capitalization and spelling out of the way, let's talk grammar.

What is grammar, anyway? When I think of grammar, I'm reminded of a poem from Walt Kelly's comic strip, *Pogo*:

"Do you herd sheep?" ol' gramma cried,

My grampa leapt in fright,

"That grammar's wrong!" to me he sighed,

"HAVE you heard sheep is right."[12]

Grammar is the word we use to describe the system that governs a language. It's a set of rules for how words, phrases, and sentences work together. Grammar for one language may be quite different from another, which my wife and I learned firsthand when we lived in China. In Mandarin, they don't conjugate (or change the tense of) verbs, which makes Mandarin easier to learn and use, once you get the hang of it. But when we adopted an older child from China, we found out it's a lot harder going from Chinese to English.

Lots of us are so bad at grammar we don't notice when someone else goofs—but we can at least avoid the most egregious examples. If you know you struggle with using correct grammar, make sure and have a grammar pro proofread your profile for you.

HOMEWORK

Check your profile for improper capitalization, spelling, and grammar—and correct your mistakes!

---

[12] Walt Kelly, "How Low Is the Lowing Herd," *Uncle Pogo So-So Stories*, 1953.

EXTRA CREDIT

Post this:

> *What's the spelling, punctuation, or grammar mistake that trips you up the most?*
>
> *For me, it's . . . [insert your mistake here].*
>
> *What about you?*

People enjoy hearing they're not alone when it comes to difficulties with language, and this post will help humanize you to your audience.

DAY 26

TURN ON CREATOR MODE

In March 2021, LinkedIn introduced "creator mode," a new suite of options that is available to everyone, but must be activated and configured. "Turning on creator mode more prominently displays your content and encourages others to follow you,"[13] wrote Margaret Rose Taormina, a Senior Product Manager at LinkedIn. According to LinkedIn, when you turn on creator mode then:

- The Connect button on your profile will change to Follow.
- LinkedIn will display the number of followers you have in your profile introduction.
- You'll be able to choose to display the topics you post about in your profile introduction.
- LinkedIn will reorder your profile to show your Featured and Activity sections first.

---

[13] See https://www.linkedin.com/pulse/introducing-creator-mode-your-linkedin-profile-margaret-rose-taormina. Accessed 16 September 2021.

- Your Activity section will be expanded to showcase more of your recent content and will no longer show your likes, comments, and other activities.[14]

LinkedIn researcher Richard van der Blom adds that the reach or engagement of your content does not increase immediately after you enable Creator Mode, but two months after you turn it on, it:

- Builds your community of followers 5 times more quickly.
- Increases your reach by +15% if your content contains the hashtags you have highlighted on your profile.
- Moves your content higher up on your LinkedIn profile.[15]

Why did LinkedIn create creator mode? "The new creator mode is likely to get more people to post on LinkedIn," reads an article about the new feature in the *Wall Street Journal*, also saying that creator mode is "a setting designed to encourage users to post more of their own original content, perhaps with an eye to becoming influencers, or in corporate-speak, thought leaders."[16]

In other words, LinkedIn wants you to create free content that will attract more people to LinkedIn. If you cooperate, LinkedIn will reward you with more attention.

---

[14] See https://www.linkedin.com/help/linkedin/answer/125388/linkedin-creator-mode. Accessed 16 September 2021.
[15] See https://www.linkedin.com/posts/richardvanderblom_linkedin-algorithm-report-edition-2021-activity-6848141573990051840-spu1. Accessed 1 October 2021.
[16] Ann-Marie Alcántara. "LinkedIn Adds 'Creator Mode' to Help More of Its Users Turn Influencers." 30 March 2021. Accessed 16 September 2021. https://www.wsj.com/articles/linkedin-adds-creator-mode-to-help-more-of-its-users-turn-influencers-11617129192.

That said, Andy Foote says, "Many established LinkedIn content creators greeted the launch of creator mode with a collective shrug. They were hoping for additional tools and analytics to understand why content succeeded or failed and to quickly figure out what their audience preferred. LinkedIn responded to this lukewarm reception of creator mode by saying that this is merely the first phase and there is more to come."

To turn on creator mode:

1. Go to your profile page, find Your Dashboard, and click "Creator mode: Off" to edit this setting.
2. Click "Next" after you see the preview of changes to be made.
3. Add one to five topics (hashtags) you post about the most. I recommend you choose the option to show these topics in your Profile Intro.
4. Click "Save."

HOMEWORK

Check your LinkedIn profile to see if creator mode is on, and if not, turn it on by following the instructions above.

EXTRA CREDIT

Your post for today:

> *Have you turned on creator mode on your LinkedIn profile? I turned it on for my profile. Here's how to do it for yours:*
>
> 1. *Go to your profile page, find Your Dashboard, and click "Creator mode: Off" to turn it to edit this setting.*
> 2. *Click "Next" after you see the preview of changes to be made.*

3. *Add one to five topics (hashtags) you post about the most. I recommend you choose the option to show these topics in your Profile Intro.*

4. *Click "Save."*

If you need any help or have any questions, let me know!

SECTION 3

MAKE MEANINGFUL CONNECTIONS

"You will be the same person in five years as you are today except for the people you meet and the books you read." — Charlie "Tremendous" Jones

When I conduct surveys on LinkedIn and ask people what their #1 goal is, the most common answer is invariably "To make meaningful connections."

What does a meaningful connection look like to you?

Here's what it *doesn't* look like. Perhaps this has happened to you. . . .

You wake up one morning to find a new request to connect on LinkedIn. You've never met this person and haven't interacted with them online, but it looks like a real person, so you decide to accept.

No sooner have you accepted the connection request then you receive an automated message with a sales pitch that is completely irrelevant to anything you're interested in. This would be obvious in two seconds to anyone who looked at your profile, so you suspect this person didn't look at yours at all.

Is that a meaningful connection, or likely to turn into one? Unlikely.

Free tip: Don't do this. It doesn't work. I once got talked into trying it—I gave it a good try—I even took great care to make sure I targeted the right people with a compelling message, and it still didn't work.

Maybe it's experiences like this that have taught people to hate networking. "The funny thing is, everyone says they hate 'networking,' but those same people will also say they love connecting with new people," says John Corcoran, former White House Writer, aide in the Clinton Administration, and co-CEO of Rise25, a lead generation agency. "What most people don't realize is that LinkedIn is a tremendous tool for launching new meaningful connections."[17]

How does he do this?

For Corcoran, it starts with delivering value. "When I connect with someone on LinkedIn, I want to immediately deliver value to them so they are left with a positive impression," he says. "It could be engaging over an upcoming industry event, or including them in an article I am writing, or interviewing them on my podcast."[18]

If you want to make meaningful connections and network the right way, treat people the way you want to be treated. Or, even better, treat them the way *they* want to be treated. Once you do, you'll be ready to maximize your influence on LinkedIn as you connect with large numbers of your ideal audience. It won't be a chore and it won't feel awkward, because you'll be doing it the right way.

---

[17] Personal communication with Josh Steimle.
[18] Personal communication with Josh Steimle.

DAY 27

CONNECT WITH LOTS OF PEOPLE

Sometimes I get flack for saying you should connect to lots of people on LinkedIn. Critics assume I am recommending you connect with anyone and everyone and focus on having as many connections as possible.

That is NOT what I'm saying.

I recommend you connect with lots of high-quality connections, meaning people you can help, and who can help you. The more of these people you connect with, the greater the good that can be generated as you serve one another.

Imagine you have a new sales technique that entrepreneurs can use to grow their businesses ten times faster. That means more people have access to their products and services, and if those products and services are desirable, then they're making the world a better place.

Let's imagine you want to be hired as a consultant to implement this revolutionary sales technique for clients, and you want to speak at marketing and sales conferences about it. However, you say, "I only connect on LinkedIn with people I've met in real life," or, "I can't possibly get to know more than one thousand people, so I won't connect with anyone beyond that."

Because you limited your connections to a small number, few people will see your posts about your super sales system. You've cut yourself off from the very people who might hire you to consult with them or speak at events.

On the other hand, let's imagine you spend the next year seeking out the people on LinkedIn who can benefit the most from what you have to share. Then you connect with them until you reach the maximum LinkedIn allows (thirty thousand connections).

Then you SPAM all of them! Bwahaha!

No, that's also NOT what I'm advocating.

Instead, imagine you connect with thirty thousand people on LinkedIn and you begin to share your knowledge freely. You tell people how your sales system works. You give away your formula, secrets, and methods. You tell them exactly how they can do what you've done, and you answer questions. Even as you give away all this value, you don't ask for anything in return. You're serving others.

What about being served? Although 99 percent of the people consuming your content will never hire you or buy from you, 1 percent will. Is that enough? If you only have three hundred connections, maybe it isn't, but it probably is if you have thirty thousand.

Connect with more people in order to serve more, even as you're being served.

HOMEWORK

First, connect with those you already know. Click on "Network" at the top of LinkedIn and upload your email contact list and connect with everyone (unless it's someone you really don't want to be connected to). Do this now, if you haven't already.

Then, go through the suggested connections LinkedIn provides for you and click "Connect" for anyone you know, who also knows you, and will be sure to accept your connection request. You don't need to customize these requests because these people know you.

Second, identify who your ideal audience is, the people you *really* want to connect with. I'll tell you how to connect with them the right way in the next chapter.

EXTRA CREDIT

Post the text below. This post will put your network to work, introducing you to valuable new connections.

When those people are tagged in the comments on your post, then it's easy for you to reach out and make a connection request, and because they were already introduced to you in the post, they'll be more likely to accept your request.

> *I'd like to connect with . . . [describe your ideal audience in one sentence].*
>
> *Who do you know who I should be connecting with?*
>
> *Please tag them in the comments below.*
>
> *Thanks!*

DAY 28

CONNECT THE RIGHT WAY

In the last chapter, I recommended you connect with everyone you already know by uploading your email list. Depending on the size of the list you uploaded, you may already have hundreds or even thousands more connections than you did twenty-four hours ago.

Because every one of those new contacts has hundreds or thousands of their own connections, this means your extended network, the one that includes people with whom you have at least one mutual connection, is expanding exponentially.

Think of it like this. . . . Imagine you have a hundred connections on LinkedIn, and each of those connections has a hundred connections that you're not already connected to. That would mean you have ten thousand second connections on LinkedIn.

Suppose you added another hundred connections, and each of them also had a hundred connections. That means you've just added another ten thousand second connections for a grand total of twenty thousand second connections.

However, according to Omnicore, the average CEO on LinkedIn has 930 connections,[19] and CEOs actually aren't the most connected bunch (they're often too busy running their businesses to think about anything else), so let's round up to 1,000. If you add 1,000 second connections each time you add a new first connection, that means that if you add a thousand connections by uploading your list, you've added a million new second connections!

Here's why this matters—if you send a connection request to someone who's a second connection, they're more likely to accept your request when they see that you know someone they know. It's even better if you have several mutual connections. This is why we start building your connections with the people you already know, so we can expand the pool of second connections you have. However, we're still not ready to connect to your ideal audience members.

Next, you'll connect with your second connections with whom you share common employment experiences, educational institutions, and LinkedIn groups. When you initiate a connection with people who have worked at the same company you have, studied at the same school, or are members of the same group, this will show up in the connection request and the recipient will be much more likely to accept your request.

After you make these requests, find second connections who share common interests. You may not have worked at the same company, but perhaps you're in the same field. Connecting with them will improve your insight into your industry and show others that you have your finger on its pulse.

---

[19] "LinkedIn by the Numbers: Stats, Demographics & Fun Facts." Accessed 16 September 2021. https://www.omnicoreagency.com/linkedin-statistics.

Finally, connect with second connections who are part of your ideal audience. By this point, you'll already have a lot of connections and your ideal audience will see this and be more likely to accept your connection request.

Customizing your invite is helpful no matter who you want to connect it, but it is especially important with this audience. When creating a unique invitation, Larry Kim, CEO of MobileMonkey, a Facebook Messenger marketing platform, recommends the "Five Ps":[20]

1. **Polite**: Recognize that the recipient is doing you a favor when they read your request, let alone respond to it.

2. **Pertinent**: Is your invitation relevant to something they need or want? How can you communicate this?

3. **Personalized**: Use their name and other details to let them know your invitation was custom-written for them, and them alone.

4. **Professional**: Leave the sailor language and bawdy jokes for the high seas.

5. **Praiseful**: Say something positive about the recipient that is relevant to why you're reaching out. (e.g., "I'm reaching out because I liked what you said on the XYZ podcast. . . ." or "Your book prompted me to connect with you. . . ."

Connecting doesn't stop when your request is accepted. Roberto Severino, a SEO consultant, shares how, after he connects with people, "Then, if they post good content I like, I will start commenting on it

---

[20] See https://mobilemonkey.com/articles/linkedin-invitation-etiquette. Accessed 28 September 2021.

with my own thoughts." Severino continues, "I'll also give people endorsements, recommendations, and so on, if I see that we're getting along well and we're a good fit."[21]

This is how you build long-term relationships on LinkedIn that will generate real results.

HOMEWORK

Continue to build your network. To summarize, connect with people in this order:

1. People you know
2. Second connections with whom you share employment, education, or groups
3. Second connections who are like you and share common interests
4. Second connections who are part of your ideal audience

You already finished #1 in the last chapter, and you can get started on the rest now. However, this is a long-term prospect, so don't expect to finish it today, or ever. As long as you're alive, you'll keep making new connections. The key today is to start down the path. And decide how you will continue to grow your network in the days and weeks to come.

---

21 Personal communication with Josh Steimle.

EXTRA CREDIT

Here's your post for the day:

> *What's the best professional compliment you've ever received, and who gave it to you?*
>
> *(feel free to tag them in the comments)*

If someone who is a second connection comments, that shows they're active on LinkedIn. These are people you want to connect with because you can use LinkedIn to serve each other.

DAY 29

BE A MATCHER

Adam Grant, researcher and author of *Give and Take*, studied more than thirty thousand professionals and found most have an abundant, sharing mentality—they help others *and* expect others will help them, and everyone comes out ahead.

These are "matchers."

Grant also discovered there are people who are pure givers, who give without asking anything. On the other end of the spectrum are takers. People in both of these groups—yes, even the givers, are less successful than matchers who see relationships as a matter of give AND take.

Givers fail because they burn out. Takers fail because everyone hates them.

Be a LinkedIn *matcher*.

HOMEWORK

1. Introduce your connections to each other, and ask for introductions.

2. Give and ask for profile recommendations.

3. Share content and create conversations.

EXTRA CREDIT

Post something like this, suggested by Lila Smith:

> *If you want to become an expert on how to use LinkedIn, @Josh Steimle [type the @ symbol then the person's name you want to tag] has written a book called* 60 Days to LinkedIn Mastery. *If you're new to LinkedIn, I'd recommend grabbing a copy and starting there! You might also want to check out [CONTACT] and [CONTACT] as examples of how others are using LinkedIn well.*
>
> *I've been learning a lot about LinkedIn from Josh's book, so if you have any questions about how to use LinkedIn, leave your comments below and I'll help if I can.*

DAY 30

BYOF (BRING YOUR OWN FOLLOWERS)

Gary Vaynerchuk is an entrepreneur and speaker—known by his sizable fan base as "Gary Vee"—who's perhaps most famous for his hustle-hustle ethic and use of colorful language. Love him or hate him (most people seem to have strong opinions one way or the other), he's pulled off success after success, and many look to him as their mentor when it comes to entrepreneurship, marketing, and social media utilization.

One thing Gary constantly talks about is moving with your audience's attention, or even anticipating where they'll go next and jumping ahead of them. Gary is a master of transferring his audience from one medium to another. He has successfully moved his YouTube audience to Twitter, his Twitter audience to Snapchat, and his Snapchat fans to Instagram. Lately, Gary has been all-in on LinkedIn.

Gary gets outsized responses to all his LinkedIn posts, routinely attracting several hundred comments on each one (average for most people is between zero and two). Why? Because he brought a ton of followers over from everywhere else he's been.

What about you—do you have followers outside of LinkedIn?

We've already talked about importing your contacts from Gmail or Outlook in previous chapters, but what about your audience on Twitter, Facebook, Instagram, or YouTube? Do you have a customer database? How about an email list?

Here are some easy ideas to bring your followers with you to LinkedIn:

- Export your customer database or email list to a CSV file and upload it to LinkedIn
- Alternatively, send an email to your email list or database and invite them to connect with you
- Promote LinkedIn activity in your email newsletters (e.g., "I asked a question on LinkedIn, I'd love to get your thoughts on it. . . .")
- Use your LinkedIn profile link as your website link on other social media profiles

These people already know you, so they are more likely to become your raving fans on LinkedIn and engage with your content. That's good, because fifty raving fans are worth more than five thousand people you don't know.

HOMEWORK

If you have an email newsletter, customer database, or other list of email addresses, upload it to LinkedIn.

Put your LinkedIn profile link anywhere it makes sense, like in your other social media profiles or your email signature.

Promote your LinkedIn activity on any other channels where you're active.

EXTRA CREDIT

Post this:

> *If LinkedIn changed to only allow one hundred connections instead of thirty thousand, who would those one hundred connections be for you?*
>
> *For me, some of those one hundred would definitely be . . . [tag five to ten people you would most want to remain connected to].*
>
> *These are people who . . . [explain why you chose those people].*
>
> *What about you? Who are some of the people who would make it onto your top one hundred and why?*

DAY 31

MUTE POSTS THAT GET IN YOUR WAY

Does that red number on your notifications icon in the upper right of the LinkedIn menu bar stress you out?

This may not be a huge problem for you right now, but if you begin to build a following on LinkedIn, people will begin to tag you in their posts. Soon, you'll go to your notifications and you won't be able to find what you want because it will be full of notifications saying, "So and so commented on a post that includes you . . ." and you'll scream "I don't care!"

Here's one way to make notifications a little less of a burden. Get rid of notifications on posts you don't care about by going to Notifications, finding a post you don't care about, clicking on the three dots on the right-hand side, and then selecting "Mute."

This means you will get zero notifications about any interaction on this post, so make sure you're OK with that before doing this.

I've found this a useful way to keep my notifications feed cleaner so I can find what I want more quickly and easily.

In addition to muting individual posts, you might also choose to not see certain types of posts.

Don't care to know when it's a connection's birthday? Make it disappear!

Indifferent about whether one of your connections has a work anniversary? Gone!

Couldn't care less that someone endorsed you for a particular skill? Out of sight, out of mind!

Simply click on "Notifications" and then "View Settings" in the upper right to turn all the notifications off.

Perhaps you think it would be nice to see notifications for all these things. In that case, turn the notifications on.

HOMEWORK

Go to your notifications and mute whatever you prefer to avoid receiving notifications about.

EXTRA CREDIT

Post this:

> *What's the most meaningful congratulation you've received on LinkedIn?*
>
> *These days social media automates wishing people a happy birthday and congratulating others on their work anniversaries, and it takes some of the meaning away when you know it can be done without much thought.*
>
> *How do you make sure the congratulations you give others mean something?*

DAY 32

REACH OUT TO LURKERS

People are visiting your LinkedIn profile and checking you out—and LinkedIn tells you exactly who they are. But are you looking at the information LinkedIn gives you? If you're looking to make high-quality, easy connections, this could be a gold mine for you.

To check out who's checking *you* out, go to your LinkedIn profile. On the left of the screen, underneath your picture and name, you'll see "Who's viewed your profile."

Click on that number and LinkedIn will show you people who've recently visited you. (The exact number you'll see depends on whether you have a paid or free version of LinkedIn.)

Between the stats at the top and the list of profiles underneath, there's an area where you can filter the profiles. One button says "interesting views." These are profiles LinkedIn thinks are noteworthy for you.

Maybe you have lots of mutual interests, or you went to the same school, or you have mutual connections, and so on. Try clicking this button and the others to see how the filters work.

To make new meaningful connections, scan the list for second connections who look interesting and worth contacting. When you find someone you want to connect with, send them a personalized connection message with something like, "Hey, I saw you looked at my LinkedIn profile recently. It looks like we have some overlapping interests. How can I help you?"

That's the speedy version. If you want to take more time and make an even higher quality introduction, look at their profile to see specific information to talk about.

When you send a connection request this way, there's a 99 percent chance they'll accept, because they're already interested in you and know who you are.

HOMEWORK

Look at who has been visiting your profile. Find five interesting people you'd like to connect with, and send them customized connection requests.

EXTRA CREDIT

Post this. It's a great way to bring recognition to some of the best people on LinkedIn, especially people who may be flying under the radar.

> *Who have you connected with recently on LinkedIn who has become a valuable part of your network?*
>
> *A little while ago I linked up with . . . [tag someone who you recently connected with and talk about why that connection has been valuable to you].*
>
> *Who's adding value to your network?*

DAY 33

JOIN GROUPS (EVEN THOUGH LINKEDIN GROUPS STINK)

As of this writing, LinkedIn groups are almost completely useless.

Due to an abundance of bugs that keep groups from working correctly and a shortage of innovation, groups have stagnated for years. People join them, but there's little to no helpful activity in most of them, even those with hundreds of thousands of members.

The easiest fix would be for LinkedIn to copy how Facebook groups work, but I'm not going to hold my breath.

There is, however, one reason why it's worth it to join LinkedIn groups. If you join a group, and then send a connection request to someone else in the same group, LinkedIn will show the other person that you're in the group with them—which will make it more likely that the person will accept your connection request.

For example, if I join the Chief Marketing Officers group, and I then try to connect with a CMO in that group, she'll see that we're both in that group and figure, "Hey, we have similar interests," and my chances of her accepting my request go way up.

Other than for this purpose, I wouldn't waste time in LinkedIn groups until they fix them, unless you're already in one that works well for you.

HOMEWORK

If you're not in any groups, find a few where your ideal audience hangs out and join them.

EXTRA CREDIT

Post this:

> *Are you in any LinkedIn groups you love?*
>
> *Some people say LinkedIn groups aren't helpful, but if you're in one that is, I'd like to know what it is that makes the group worth your time.*
>
> *For me, the most valuable group I'm in is . . . [skip this last part if you're not in any groups you find valuable].*

DAY 34

TAKE IT OFFLINE WITH EVENTS

A few years ago, Anna McAfee, a LinkedIn trainer, invited her friends via LinkedIn to join her at a coffee shop in Coffs Harbour, Australia. She called it "LinkedIn Local." Her event was successful, but it went further than that small meeting at the cafe. Within hours, others who had seen Anna's post were organizing their own LinkedIn Local events around the world.

Not long after, I had the chance to sit down with Alexandra Galviz, aka "Authentic Alex," who held the first LinkedIn Local event in London. She told me how the events were "completely organic" but tapped into a desire many people on LinkedIn had to meet their connections in person.

On LinkedIn, we all have dozens, hundreds, or even thousands of "weak" connections, or people we don't really know that well, if at all. However, when you meet someone in person whom you previously only knew through LinkedIn, it creates a strong connection.

LinkedIn Local events grew to more than 350 cities in 96 countries before LinkedIn absorbed them and . . . kind of squashed them. "If only LinkedIn had seen its potential, a way to track it, a way to support it," Anna recently posted.

A recent survey showed 60 percent of business leaders believe in-person events are "the most critical marketing channel for achieving business goals."[22] In light of the recent global pandemic, live events were largely put on hold, but that has made them only that much more important as many suffer from loneliness and a lack of in-person connection.[23]

People may go back to holding LinkedIn Local events once things get more normal post-pandemic—or they may not. The real point is that many of the people you know on LinkedIn would love to meet you in person, as well as meet *each other* in person. Be the one to facilitate this, or join an existing event.

How easy is it to take LinkedIn offline? Just post that you're hosting an event at a local cafe, a hotel lobby, or a park, and then show up. You don't have to do anything fancy. Create an event to:

- Learn from an expert you invite (or perhaps you are the expert)
- Listen to a panel discussion
- Organize a business book club
- Or grab a bite to eat and chat with no set agenda.

If you want to be more organized, use LinkedIn Events to attract attendees, manage signups, and share information. LinkedIn Events allows you to make a meetup public or private (invite only, or only accessible to those with the hidden URL) and send out invitations through LinkedIn (up to a thousand). People don't have to be connected to you to register for an event.

---

[22] "Event Marketing 2020: Benchmarks and Trends Report." Bizzabo. Accessed 16 September 2021. https://welcome.bizzabo.com/reports/event-marketing-2020.
[23] Taylor Lorenz. "Now Going Viral: Meeting Online Friends in Real Life." *New York Times.* 15 August 2021. Accessed 16 September 2021. https://www.nytimes.com/2021/08/15/technology/tik-tok-friends-meet-up.html.

HOMEWORK

Find an in-person event through LinkedIn and attend it.

EXTRA CREDIT

Host an event! To make it as easy as possible to host your first one, here's a post that can start things off:

> *I'd love to meet you in person! I'm going to be at . . . [safe, public location] on . . . [date] at . . . [time].*
>
> *If you want to come and hang out and talk LinkedIn or . . . [list some of your professional interests], I'd love to see you there!*
>
> *Comment below if you're going to come. If a lot of people respond, I'll make sure the venue can handle all of us.*

When you host an offline event, not only will you strengthen the connections you already have, your event is likely to attract a number of people you don't know, who you can then add to your LinkedIn network.

DAY 35

USE LINKEDIN LIVE TO ATTRACT CONNECTIONS

When much of the world shut down to in-person events in 2020 due to the global pandemic, companies that allowed people to connect online saw a surge of growth. During the three months leading through January 2021, everyone's favorite online conference software, Zoom, saw its revenues grow a whopping 369 percent from the previous quarter (in which they had already seen triple-digit growth).[24]

Likewise, LinkedIn prospered during the pandemic, with 50 percent year-on-year growth in content sharing from 2019 to 2020. A significant portion of that growth was due to a relatively new tool called LinkedIn Live which itself saw an 89 percent increase in usage between March and June of 2020.[25]

---

[24] Daniel Newman. "Opinion: Zoom's pandemic-fueled growth is the start, not the end." *MarketWatch*. Accessed 16 September 2021. https://www.marketwatch.com/story/zooms-pandemic-fueled-growth-is-the-start-not-the-end-11622641279.

[25] Darain Faraz. "Working It Out, Together." *Linkedin Official Blog*. Accessed 16 September 2021. https://blog.linkedin.com/2020/august/5/working-it-out-together.

LinkedIn Live allows you to stream live video through LinkedIn. Video streams are automatically displayed in the feeds of those who follow you, and if you set up a LinkedIn Event to promote your LinkedIn Live, people can sign up ahead of time to participate. As viewers watch you, they can interact with you and other viewers in the comments section. When you finish the stream, it's archived as a video post.

LinkedIn Live originally launched in February 2019 to a limited number of users. In 2020, LinkedIn tied LinkedIn Events and LinkedIn Live together, effectively creating a complete virtual events solution. Since February 2020, LinkedIn Live streams have grown by 158 percent.[26]

Why should you host a LinkedIn Live stream? Because LinkedIn Live videos attract a high level of engagement. Native video is fantastic, but according to LinkedIn, LinkedIn Live generates seven times the reactions and twenty-four times more comments.[27] If you've ever hosted a webinar before, using LinkedIn Live is similar. And since the pandemic forced us all to become expert users with Zoom, the idea of talking to an audience via live video should be familiar.

When you host a LinkedIn Live stream, you'll connect more deeply with your existing network, and you'll also attract people who have never heard of you before.

---

[26] *Linkedin Pressroom.* "LinkedIn Business Highlights from Microsoft's FY20 Q3 Earnings." Accessed 16 September 2021. https://news.linkedin.com/2020/april/linkedin-business-highlights-from-microsoft-s-fy20-q3-earnings.

[27] *Linkedin Marketing Solutions.* "LinkedIn Live." Accessed 16 September 2021. https://business.linkedin.com/marketing-solutions/linkedin-live.

HOMEWORK

Here are the basic steps to get started using LinkedIn Live:

1. **Apply for LinkedIn Live at https://www.linkedin.com/help/linkedin/ask/lv-app.** As of this writing, LinkedIn Live isn't available to everyone. After you apply, you may have to wait a few days or even weeks to find out if your application is accepted (all the more reason to do it now).

2. **Choose a third-party streaming tool.** LinkedIn doesn't yet stream natively, so you have to use a tool like StreamYard, Socialive, Restream, or Switcher. (Access a full, updated list of third-party tools you can use with LinkedIn Live in my free Ultimate LinkedIn Mastery Resource List at BlueMethod.io/list.)

   Note: In January 2021, StreamYard was acquired by the startup Hopin, which received a substantial investment from LinkedIn in June 2021, so there's a good chance StreamYard is going to be a good long-term solution for streaming to LinkedIn Live.[28] Coauthor *Andy Foote adds, "I personally prefer StreamYard because it gives me a good balance of ease-of-use and customization. The StreamYard cofounders also stream a weekly town hall and are very good at supporting their users."*

3. **Connect LinkedIn to your third-party tool.** Each tool has an area to connect it to your LinkedIn account. It will be in a different place depending on the tool, but look around and you'll find it.

---

[28] Ari Levy. "LinkedIn bets on remote events, investing in $5 billion-plus virtual platform company Hopin." 9 June 2021. Accessed 18 September 2021. https://www.cnbc.com/2021/06/09/linkedin-invests-in-hopin-betting-on-post-pandemic-remote-events.html.

4. **Choose your company page or personal profile.** Stream your LinkedIn Live video through a company page or your personal profile. Andy Foote says, "I run my LinkedIn Live shows via my personal profile because I believe folks generally prefer to engage with me personally, rather than with my company page brand." That said, if you have spent a lot of time and effort building an audience and presence via your company page, it would make sense to run your Live stream from your company page.

5. **Go live or schedule your stream for later.** To broadcast immediately, write a title and description and then go live. However, in most cases I'd recommend you schedule your stream in advance. This will give you time to promote it through LinkedIn Events and other channels like your email newsletter or other social media accounts. In StreamYard's case, you can create a LinkedIn Event for your stream within the tool (no need to create the event separately through LinkedIn). Functionality in other tools varies.

   Note: If you set up an event in LinkedIn, rather than through a third-party tool like StreamYard, LinkedIn will ask for a "Registration or broadcast link." To get this link, log into your third-party tool where you scheduled the stream and then copy the URL the tool created for the stream. Paste the URL into your LinkedIn event page.

6. **Promote your LinkedIn Live.** Once you create an event through these tools, promote it through LinkedIn as well as other channels. Posting about an upcoming Live stream, scheduling it as an event with plenty of notice, using all of the available tools to generate interest and buzz (e.g., polls, document posts, comments, etc.) on LinkedIn and on other social channels are all great ways to ensure live viewership.

7. **Go live!** This can be nerve-wracking the first time, so you may want to do a smaller event or a practice run before you do something more critical. None of the 3rd party streaming tools lets you do a practice run/simulated livestream, so accept that your first livestream will probably begin with you looking blankly at the camera and asking "Are we live?" You will make mistakes. The key is to learn as quickly as possible what not to do, in that first session.

EXTRA CREDIT

Is LinkedIn Live the right fit for you? That partly depends on you, and partly it depends on your audience. To find out if your audience is interested in seeing you go live, post this:

I'm thinking of doing a LinkedIn Live stream, but first:

1. *Have you ever attended a LinkedIn Live stream?*
2. *What was good about it? What could have been better?*
3. *If I did a LinkedIn Live stream, what would you like to see and hear from me?*

Try that out and you'll likely get some helpful comments.

SECTION 4

CREATE COMPELLING CONTENT

Congratulations! Your profile is now optimized and you've built a strong network of meaningful, high-quality connections. The next step (although you've been doing it since the beginning of this book), is to create content for your ideal audience that moves them to action.

But what should you post? Whatever works for you and your audience.

If you feel handicapped as a writer, but video is easy for you, then do video. If you create business cartoons, post those images. If you're a master at slide presentations, export those as PDFs and post them as documents.

Focus on the type of content that comes easily to you and gives you energy; otherwise you'll burn out and quit.

However, also take into account what LinkedIn likes. As of this writing, LinkedIn likes relatively short posts that are plain text and native video.

Graphics or images generally don't perform well in posts, and links to external articles or videos perform the worst, likely because LinkedIn doesn't want you sending traffic away from their site. Articles—the blog-length posts that can include images, formatted text, and active links—also don't attract much attention on LinkedIn, although they once did and someday they may reign supreme again.

LinkedIn Carousels—clickable slideshows—had their moment in the sun, but, as of this writing, says my coauthor Aaron Wrixon, they seem to have fallen out of favor as an of-the-moment fad.

LinkedIn is fickle and its team is constantly changing the algorithm, so what works today may not work tomorrow—and what works for one person may not work as well for another. The only constant is change, and the only antidote is to continually experiment and adapt. Create the content that works for you, and if it stops working, try something else.

That said, this section contains many tips based on timeless principles that will make your content shine, no matter what changes LinkedIn has in store.

DAY 36

SLAY THE SAME DRAGON EVERY DAY

When I was contributing articles to *Forbes*, one of their editors counseled writers to "Slay the same dragon every day."

From that editor's perspective, the writers whose articles were the most popular and who built the largest followings stuck to a single topic and dug into that topic each and every day—while avoiding unrelated fields.

At the time, I was NOT slaying the same dragon every day. Each time I wrote, I created content that had nothing to do with my last article. My writing was all over the place, depending on what I was interested in that day.

Then I got focused, and man, oh man, did my life ever change. I went from being "that guy who writes interesting stuff sometimes" to "that marketing expert guy who wrote the CMO book, and speaks at marketing conferences everywhere, and was invited to hang out with some of the top marketers in the world on Richard Branson's island, and has a marketing agency you should hire." When I focused on writing about marketing, I became known as "The Marketing Guy."

Seems like common sense, but it's a lesson I had to learn over and over.

Don't do what I did.

Instead, focus on your genius zone and go out and slay that same dragon every day on LinkedIn.

Your dragon will change over time. It's good to be consistent, but if you switch careers or reinvent yourself then of course your audience and content may change as well.

HOMEWORK

Look at the last five posts you created on LinkedIn.

If someone had to figure out what you're all about based on nothing but those posts, would they have a good idea of who you are, what you do, and who you do it for?

Would they know how to refer business to you?

Would they know how to tell you about a job that's the perfect fit for you?

If not, go back and review Day 4: Find Your Genius Zone. With every post you write, ask yourself, "Does this post build my personal brand around my genius zone, or will it distract people from my genius zone?"

Slay that dragon!

EXTRA CREDIT

Post this:

> *What's your dragon?*
>
> *A* Forbes *editor once said that if you want to be a successful writer you should "slay the same dragon every day."*

My dragon is . . . [talk about your focus].

What's your dragon?

DAY 37

DON'T TALK ABOUT WHAT YOU DON'T KNOW

When writing content for LinkedIn, it's easy to stray into areas where you are neither a genius nor an expert and make a fool of yourself in the process (trust me, I know).

When you talk about what you *don't* know, you:

- Alienate your ideal audience
- Waste time
- Lose credibility
- Diminish your effectiveness
- Develop a personal brand as an amateur

This doesn't mean you have to know more than *anyone* else about your topic before you can say *anything*, but you need to know enough. However, "enough" is a relative term. If you're going to talk about brain development, brain plasticity, and neural regeneration and repair fields, like Andrew Huberman does on the Huberman Lab podcast, it helps to be a tenured professor in the Department of Neurobiology at the Stanford University School of Medicine.

If Huberman is an extreme example of knowing what you're talking about, I was on the other extreme when I was asked to write a column in a trail running magazine. It was 2014, and I wasn't an expert runner of any sort, and had only begun to experiment with trail running. The only reason the editor asked me to write for his magazine was because he knew I enjoyed writing.

When I told the editor I didn't think I knew enough about trail running to write a column, and that I was afraid of giving people incorrect information and making myself look like an idiot, he said, "That's ok, you'll write the beginner's column."

That was something I could handle. I came up with a list of questions I had about trail running (and as a beginner myself, I had a lot), and each month I chose a question, researched it until I was confident I had the right answer, and then I wrote an article about it using a tone that said, "I'm here with you, I barely learned this myself."

Like me with trail running, even if you have little to no expertise on a topic, establish yourself as an expert by being the person who is new to the field, learning alongside your audience, and sharing what you find out.

Another way to become a recognized expert in your field is to interview the established experts. This can produce great video content for LinkedIn, as well as text posts. As you interview the top experts, you'll be a beneficiary of guilt by association, and of course, you'll also learn a lot in the process and become a true expert in your own right.

HOMEWORK

As you're creating content, ask yourself, "Do I really know what I'm talking about here?" If not, find a way to learn what you need to know to be a true expert. Regardless of your level of expertise, use a tone of humility to better appeal to your audience.

EXTRA CREDIT

Post this:

> *What do you know?*
>
> *I once was advised, "Write about what you know."*
>
> *I know . . . [talk about what you know, i.e., your genius zone].*
>
> *What's your area of expertise?*

DAY 38

DON'T TALK POLITICS ON LINKEDIN

I could have included this in the earlier list of "don't do this on LinkedIn" items, but it deserves its own chapter, especially as politics have become more divisive than ever.

I'm a politics junkie with strong opinions, but as a general rule, I don't share them on LinkedIn. LinkedIn isn't where I go to debate or sound off on matters of government policy.

My purpose on LinkedIn is to serve others and assist them in their professional roles. If I were to share my perspectives on politics, I'd lose at least half my audience. Even those who agree with me politically would say, "Why is he sharing this stuff here? I'm not on LinkedIn to read *this*." *Then* who would I be serving?

Unless you have a *really* good reason, stay away from politics.

Sometimes it will be difficult. The global pandemic brought political matters into the office in ways that were hard to ignore. Still, for the vast majority of people on LinkedIn, posting about politics or anything else that is controversial is high-risk with a low reward. I'm all about taking risks and experimenting, but there are some risks not worth taking. If you read or hear something about politics and feel you simply MUST share it—do it somewhere else.

HOMEWORK

Easiest homework assignment ever? Depends on if you're the type of person who feels they *have* to share their opinion on political matters. The next time you find yourself tempted to wade into a quagmire with a political post on LinkedIn . . . don't.

EXTRA CREDIT

Post this, and buckle up to watch what kind of reaction you get.

> *Does politics have a place on LinkedIn? Yes or no?*
>
> *What's your vote?*

DAY 39

GET MORE COMMENTS BY ASKING QUESTIONS

If you want your LinkedIn posts to be seen by more people, you need to get comments. There's nothing wrong with views and likes, but comments are what tell LinkedIn that people are really interested in a post. If the algorithm sees a post getting lots of comments, it will show that post to more people, leading to even more comments, and even more people seeing it, and so on.

So how do you get people to comment on your LinkedIn posts?

Through hundreds of experiments and by analyzing LinkedIn posts, both those with a lot of comments as well as those with very few, I've been able to figure out which posts tend to consistently attract a lot of comments.

If you want to get people commenting on your LinkedIn posts, then:

1. Ask a question. Ask a question at the beginning of your post, and ask the same question at the end.

2. Invite discussion. Reading a lot of LinkedIn posts, my response is "OK, so what?" Even if I want to comment on the post, I can't figure out what to say beyond "Great post!" Adding "Tell me what you think in the comments," to the end

of your post invites discussion, and it will force you to write posts that attract comments.

3. Use triggers your audience will respond to. These may be certain words, phrases, or ideas. Starting a post with, "As an entrepreneur, I think . . ." will get the attention of other entrepreneurs better than merely saying, "I think. . . ."

4. Be ready to listen (and appear to be doing so). Asking a question helps with that, as does using words that convey a tone of open-mindedness. Sometimes demonstrating uncertainty can be a great tactic, as when you say, "I'm trying to figure out XYZ, what do you think?"

There's one more tip for getting lots of comments and visibility on your posts, but it's so important it needs a day of its own, so once you're done with the action items here, flip ahead to Day 40!

HOMEWORK

What's a common question you get in your line of work? Create a LinkedIn post starting and ending with that question, and answer it yourself in between. Invite others to share their answers to the same question, and if you want to give your post an extra boost tag five to ten people who you can depend on to give great responses.

By the way, answering questions is good for more than LinkedIn, it's also a great marketing strategy to use on your website, in email newsletters, and when you're speaking. Learn more about this tactic by reading *They Ask, You Answer* by Marcus Sheridan, *#AskGaryVee* by Gary Vaynerchuk, or *Youtility* by Jay Baer.

EXTRA CREDIT

Post this:

> *What's the most common question you get asked about your job or business?*
>
> *For me, it's . . . [put the question here].*
>
> *I'll answer that question in the comments, but I'm curious about you—what question do you get asked all the time and what's the answer?*

DAY 40

RESPOND TO COMMENTS

Want your LinkedIn posts to go viral? Then respond to people who comment on them—and respond quickly.

LinkedIn wants you to spend lots of time on their website and in their app. The more time you spend there, the more likely you are to spend money on LinkedIn.

This knowledge is your secret weapon for LinkedIn success. If you help other people spend more time on LinkedIn, LinkedIn will push more people your way. If LinkedIn sees a post of yours that's attracting attention and getting people talking by leaving comments, they'll promote that post because it's keeping people on LinkedIn longer.

This is why it kills me, KILLS ME, when I see someone write a great post, and then two or three people comment on it, and the author of the post . . . never responds. Because the author never responds, the conversation dies, and an opportunity is lost!

Keep the conversation going by responding with five or more words. It's best to respond quickly, within minutes. Within the first two hours is the next window of opportunity, but even if it's several hours or days later, any response is better than no response.

"It's important to remember that people took the time to share their thoughts with you on your post; the least you can do is respond back to them," says LinkedIn coach Lacey Abbacchi. "When you do this, not only are you building a very engaged audience, but you're pushing your post further out into the feed where the algorithm will pick it up and show it to more people. If you can't respond to comments, then don't post! It's as simple as that."[29]

HOMEWORK

Create a new post, and be prepared to get into a conversation.

As soon as someone comments, respond—and if at all possible, include a question in your response so they will respond again. See how many times you can pass the conversation back and forth.

EXTRA CREDIT

Post this:

> *What questions do you have about . . . [your industry, product, etc.]?*
>
> *No sales pitch here, I'm going to answer questions and be as helpful as possible.*
>
> *Ask away, and I'll answer quickly.*
>
> *Anything goes.*

---

[29] Personal communication with Josh Steimle.

DAY 41

TELL A STORY

If you want to win on LinkedIn, learn to tell stories. A story doesn't need to be long. You may have heard the one that goes, "For sale: baby shoes. Never worn." While the legend that says Ernest Hemingway wrote the story to win a bet is likely untrue, the fact remains that regardless of the author, these six words say a lot. You can say a lot with even fewer words. Here are all the places to tell your stories:

- Your headline
- Your banner
- Your bio/summary
- Your work experience
- Your posts

People are hardwired to love stories, so tell them everywhere on LinkedIn. My kids constantly ask me to tell them stories—and we don't stop asking for them when we grow up. We read books. We watch shows and movies. We gossip. When we meet someone we haven't seen for awhile we say, "What have you been up to?"

I learned the magic of stories going to church as a little kid. I don't know what your church is like, but at mine (I'm a member of The Church of Jesus Christ of Latter-day Saints) an important part of every

Sunday meeting is listening to normal members of the congregation give talks for the better part of an hour.

Some people in my church give talks that sound like a university lecture. Others tell stories. One of these types of talks used to put me to sleep as a kid. The other kind held my attention as though with an iron fist. Can you guess which kept me awake?

I don't remember many of the thousands of talks I heard growing up, but I still remember the story of "The Big Purple Gorilla," as told by Bishop Baker. The story took ten minutes to tell, I was five years old, and I only heard the story once, but to this day it's never left me. (If you want to hear it, you'll have to ask me in person.)

HOMEWORK

Incorporate a story into your About section. It can be one sentence, or take up your entire bio.

If you're not sure where to start, type, "Once upon a time . . ." and complete the sentence.

Tell us who you are, what you do, who you do it for, *why* you do it, and the journey that brought you to where you are today.

My coauthor Aaron Wrixon recommends reading *Building a StoryBrand* by Donald Miller. In it, Miller describes a simple seven-step process to improve your marketing by telling stories that resonate with your customers or clients, which can be summarized as follows:

1. A character . . .
2. With a problem . . .
3. Meets a guide . . .
4. Who gives them a plan . . .

5. That calls them to action . . .

6. And tells them what success looks like if they follow the plan . . .

7. And what failure looks like if they don't.

In this framework, the character isn't "you," it's your audience, customer, or client. They're the hero, and you're the guide. If your audience is Luke Skywalker, you are Ben Kenobi. If your customer is Harry Potter, you are Dumbledore.

Make your customer the hero of the stories you tell, with you as the trusted advisor. They'll beat down your door for more.

How can you tell your story on LinkedIn in a way that helps your audience see themselves as heroes?

EXTRA CREDIT

Post this:

> *I was challenged to share my professional story in a post on LinkedIn. Here it is. . . .*
>
> *[Briefly, tell us who you are, what you do, who you do it for, and how you got here.]*
>
> *What's your story?*

DAY 42

POST NATIVE VIDEO

When LinkedIn launched the ability to post native video (video that is uploaded to LinkedIn and hosted here, rather than a link to a video on YouTube or something), it wanted to incentivize users to create video, so the company gave it more prominence, showing video to more people than other types of content.

Because most people are afraid to make videos, there's still a lot of opportunity. If you post videos, you will gain attention rapidly. Want proof? Try this.

Grab your phone, point it at yourself, and record a two-minute video answering these questions:

- What's your name?
- What do you do?
- Who do you do it for? (I mean your customers, not your employer.)
- What do you love about what you do?

Then end with, "Know someone I can help? Tag them in the comments."

Film it directly from LinkedIn, or record it on your phone and then upload the video file.

I did something similar once when I was living in China. I filmed a short video for LinkedIn while I was walking up a street to go meet a friend for lunch. I pulled out my phone, thought for a second, and started recording myself talking about why I had moved to China and what I was doing there. I then invited other foreigners in China, like myself, to comment on why they were in China.

That video went to more than three hundred thousand views with hundreds of comments. It also landed me a client.

One of my favorite examples of proper use of native video on LinkedIn comes from Mark Gaisford, cofounder of Redsprout Media, a content marketing agency. In 2019, Mark began to create short, humorous videos that spoke to office life and the "joys" of running a business. The videos weren't professionally produced, but they were smart and punchy. When I reached out to compliment Mark on one of his videos, he told me, "Not my usual style but it does seem to have resonated with people," and then followed up, "Nine thousand new followers in a matter of days. Crazy!"

Today, Mark continues to produce short videos that are humorous and helpful, and his follower count is more than seventy thousand. That means every time he posts a video, it immediately gets lots of comments, which helps it reach even more people.

HOMEWORK

Create that one- to two-minute video as described above.

Don't worry about lighting—just go stand outside, or near a window.

Don't worry about your hair, makeup, or how you're dressed—as long as you're decent.

Don't worry about how you sound or look.

Film it. Post it. See what happens.

Pro tip: Put captions on your videos. According to a Verizon/Publicis study, 69 percent of mobile users watch video muted in public spaces, and even in private spaces 25 percent of video viewers keep the sound off.[30] Use services like Rev.com, ClipScribe, or Descript to transcribe your video quickly and create an .srt file (find more tools in my free Ultimate LinkedIn Mastery Resource List at BlueMethod.io/list). When you upload your video to LinkedIn, click on the pencil icon to add the .srt file. Fast and easy.

EXTRA CREDIT

Post this:

> *Have you posted a video on LinkedIn?*
>
> *I don't mean sharing a YouTube link—I mean have you used the LinkedIn app to film, or created a video and then uploaded it to LinkedIn? Why or why not?*
>
> *What has your experience been like?*

---

[30] See https://adtechb2b.yahooinc.com/c/verizon-media-sound--1?x=vOJKbY. Accessed 2 October 2021.

DAY 43

PLAN

When I was a kid, my dad often said, "If you fail to plan, you plan to fail."

When it comes to creating thought leadership content on LinkedIn, follow this plan:

1. Define an objective or vision for what you want to accomplish on LinkedIn during the next month.

2. Find the genius zone that will help you make your vision a reality.

3. Identify your ideal audience, the one that can help you make your vision come to life.

4. Create compelling content that will hook the attention of your audience and call them to take the appropriate action.

5. Put reminders in your calendar so you don't forget to post.

6. Find others to work with. See Day 45 for more ideas on collaborating to expand your reach.

7. Don't forget the love. If you're in this for the right reasons and truly want to help others, it will show, and people will respond.

HOMEWORK

Create a plan.

You've heard of the KISS method? "Keep it simple, stupid."

I like that, except my mom taught me to never call people stupid. My revised version is:

> KISS = Keep it super simple.

What will your simple plan be?

Remember, if you succeed in planning, you plan to succeed. Maybe that doesn't have quite the same ring to it as what my father told me, but you get the idea.

EXTRA CREDIT

Post this:

> *How do you plan your professional life, whether it's daily, weekly, monthly, or longer term?*
>
> *My method is . . . [share how you plan your work, content, day, or anything else].*
>
> *I'd love to know what methods, tools, and technology you use to help you plan your work or life.*

DAY 44

USE #HASHTAGS

A hashtag (aka pound sign or octothorpe) isn't anything to be afraid of. It's just another punctuation mark. When you type that hashtag on Twitter, Instagram, Facebook, or LinkedIn, it becomes a way to categorize and link content.

On Twitter and Instagram, hashtags are used frequently. They make a difference on those networks *because* people use them. On Facebook, they're almost non-existent. For one reason or another, they haven't caught on there.

What about hashtags on LinkedIn? They may not be as popular as they are on Twitter and Instagram, but they are used frequently and LinkedIn seems committed to promoting them. Using a hashtag will not make the difference between your post getting fifty views and five hundred, however, there are times when hashtags are still worth using:

- When you have a series. When I first published the series that turned into this book, I used the hashtag, #LinkedIndailytip to make it easy for people to click on that and see all the other tips.
- When you want to "newsjack." If something comes out in the news and you want to create content to piggyback on it, this is when there will be real traffic going to relevant hashtags.

- When you want to highlight a word. If I'm posting that I am coming to New York because I'm going to speak there, then I'll put #NewYork at the beginning of my post to draw attention because the hashtag turns bold and blue. Use this cautiously, however, because it can also signal to LinkedIn that anyone not interested in New York won't care much about your post. (Of course, if you're going to New York and that's what you're talking about then that's probably the case anyway.)

My rule of thumb is to not stress too much about hashtags, but insert a few if it's quick and makes sense.

HOMEWORK

Use hashtags in your posts for the next week and see what happens.

Note: Richard van der Blom's annual roundup of LinkedIn algorithm updates for 2021 explains that three to five hashtags works best in a post.[31]

Make sure every hashtag is highly relevant to the content of your post.

EXTRA CREDIT

Post this and see what your audience has to say about hashtags.

> *Do you use hashtags in your LinkedIn posts? Yes or no?*
>
> *Why or why not?*
>
> *#linkedinquestions #linkedin #linkedintips*

---

[31] See https://www.linkedin.com/posts/richardvanderblom_linkedin-algorithm-report-edition-2021-activity-6848141573990051840-spu1. Accessed 2 October 2021.

DAY 45

COLLABORATE

Working alone is hard. Working with others will increase your influence on LinkedIn (and everywhere else).

Here are three ideas to help you collaborate with others to create LinkedIn success:

- **Create content together.** Allen Gannett, author of *The Creative Curve*, made a name for himself by doing short, three to five minute video interviews with interesting people and posting the videos to LinkedIn. Those he interviewed were grateful for the exposure and promoted his content, giving him more exposure. And being seen with interesting people made Allen interesting, benefitting his personal brand.

- **Engage with each others' content.** Join forces with those who comment frequently on your posts by returning the favor. This will help each others' content get more traction.

- **Tag others.** Invite those with a relevant viewpoint to comment on your posts by tagging them. (Do NOT tag the same people over and over in all your posts, and make sure to tag people who will respond—if people ignore you tagging them, this will lead your posts to be marked as spam by the LinkedIn algorithm.)

If you'd like to read more about how to collaborate effectively with others, check out these books:

- *Big Potential* by Shawn Achor
- *The Founder's Dilemmas* by Noam Wasserman
- *Rocket Fuel* by Gino Wickman (This is a must-read if you're about to start a company or take on a partner)
- *Give and Take* by Adam Grant
- *Scrum* by Jeff Sutherland (I found this book so important for my business I read it four times in three days)

HOMEWORK

To identify potential collaborators, answer the following questions:

- Who do you share your genius zone with? What other experts do exactly what you're doing? You may think of these individuals as competitors, but are there ways to work together and both come out ahead?
- Who do you share expert zones with? They may not be doing exactly what you're doing, but their knowledge and experience overlap with yours.
- Who else is targeting your ideal audience? They may or may not compete with you, but because you have the same audience, there may be a win-win opportunity.
- Are there any other individuals, groups, companies, or organizations that come to mind as collaboration opportunities for content?

EXTRA CREDIT

Earlier in this book I talked about your audience. Post this to find out who in your LinkedIn network is also targeting that same audience. (This is a great post in which to tag a few people you believe may be potential collaborators.)

> *Who's your ideal audience? If you could push a button on a vending machine and get a thousand additional customers of any type you want, what would that ideal customer look like?*
>
> *For me, the ideal customer would be . . . [talk about your ideal audience].*
>
> *If you and I have the same ideal customer, we should talk.*
>
> *But even if your audience is totally different from mine, I'd love to hear about it in the comments below, because perhaps I know others in my network who target the same people you target, and there may be an opportunity to collaborate.*

DAY 46

CONSIDER USING EMOJIS

Is it unprofessional to use emojis on LinkedIn?

When I first started to write this book, this chapter included the statement, "I wouldn't use emojis on my profile in a million years." However, the other day, I added one. Perhaps times are changing and I'm changing with them, but then, as now, my advice remains the same:

Do what works.

There's nothing right or wrong about using emojis. Whether to do so or not is all about who your audience is, and how they would react.

I believe that excessive use of emojis would alienate my audience and have a negative effect on my personal brand. However, your audience may be different from mine. They may see an emoji as perfectly professional and no problem whatsoever. They might even be attracted to your use of them.

If you're not sure whether to include emojis on your profile or in your posts, ask your followers. It's a great opportunity for a LinkedIn post to get people talking back and forth, and you may learn a lot about how your audience regards emoji use.

Pro tip: Mads Monsen, a quality assurance expert, puts an emoji in front of his name as a spam-prevention tool. "Spammers will grab the name with the emoji when sending an automated DM," he says, whereas, "A real human would not bother copying the emoji, so it acts as a spam identifier."[32]

HOMEWORK

During the next few days, look for emojis on LinkedIn. Do they feel natural to you? Do you feel like they make the person using them look unprofessional, or are they helpful in communicating ideas and feelings?

EXTRA CREDIT

Post this. It should get a good debate going.

> *How do you feel about using emojis on LinkedIn? Do you think they're never appropriate? Always appropriate? Appropriate in some places, but not in others, like your headline?*
>
> *I'd love to hear your thoughts.*

This type of question is also a good opportunity to create a LinkedIn poll.

[32] Personal communication with Josh Steimle.

DAY 47

ISSUE A CHALLENGE

People love a good challenge.

I once created a post challenging my LinkedIn network to create their first LinkedIn video. I told them to tag me in their post, promising to check out their videos and leave feedback.

During the next week, dozens of people posted videos and tagged me. I congratulated them all and gave the feedback I promised.

The posts were great publicity for their authors—and for me, too, since those people directed traffic and credit for their first video to me.

But the real payoff was the depth of connection with my audience this created. Each of these people expressed gratitude for the challenge. Some talked about how filming this first video had changed their entire perspective on LinkedIn.

The challenge you issue should relate to your purpose on LinkedIn and your area of expertise so that as people accept the challenge, you both benefit.

For example, if your expertise is sales, you might ask others to tell you their greatest fears related to sales, and challenge them to do something today to face their fears and then write a post about it and tag you in it.

Or if you're a job-seeker—let's say you're a copywriter—you could share some simple rules of great copywriting and challenge others to create a LinkedIn post while following those rules. This would further cement your expert status as a copywriter.

If you're an entrepreneur helping brands find influencers to promote their products, you could challenge your LinkedIn audience to find a way to fit an influencer into their marketing plan, even if they're a B2B brand, and share their thoughts.

When you issue a challenge and people accept it, their thinking changes. Their lives change. And when their lives change, they are reminded of you every time they see results from the change they've made.

HOMEWORK

Challenge your audience. They'll thank you for it.

EXTRA CREDIT

Post this:

> *I've got two questions I'd love for you to answer in the comments below:*
>
> 1. *Who is someone who has had a powerful influence on your life?*
> 2. *Did that person ever challenge you? If so, what did they challenge you to do?*
>
> *Someone who had a great impact on my life is . . . [tell your story].*
>
> *They challenged me to . . . [talk about what they challenged you to do, and how you benefited because of that challenge].*
>
> *Who influenced you by challenging you to do more or be more?*

DAY 48

CUT THE BUZZWORDS

Which buzzwords annoy you the most?

Let's start with ecosystem, sync, ideation, robust, pain point, leverage, bandwidth, game-changer, double-click, dogfood, iterate, sunset, bleeding edge, alignment, revolutionary, and deliverables . . . and the list goes on.

In 2018, LinkedIn published a list of ten overused buzzwords including, specialized, experienced, leadership, skilled, passionate, expert, motivated, creative, strategic, and successful.

I especially dislike the buzzword "disrupt." Don't use this word unless you've read Clayton Christensen's books *The Innovator's Dilemma* and *The Innovator's Solution*, and you know what the word "disrupt" *really* means. It's also OK to use the word if you're talking about how your coworker enters meetings late.

Similarly, I'm not a fan of how people misuse the term "growth hack."

When Tim Draper said, "Let's put a link at the bottom of every Hotmail inviting others to sign up for a free Hotmail account," *that* was a growth hack. However, many people think growth-hacking describes any form of clever marketing.

But I digress.

The alleged benefit of buzzwords is that they make you sound intelligent, but they can also make your audience feel stupid, which isn't your intent, right?

Do buzzwords and jargon have a place? Yes, when your audience uses the words like you do—and they facilitate communication.

Here's a rule of thumb that serves me well: If I think there's even a remote chance I might have to explain a word to my audience on LinkedIn, I don't use it. I simply say what I mean.

HOMEWORK

Review the content on your profile to make sure it's free of unnecessary buzzwords, and then make sure as you create new content you make it simple and buzzword-free.

EXTRA CREDIT

Post this:

> *What are some of your least favorite buzzwords?*
>
> *Are there any buzzwords you can't stop using?*

DAY 49

BE CLEAR

Try really, really hard—almost always, if not every time—to avoid, at all costs, adding lots of words that simply eat up your character count on your LinkedIn posts and that means your content is full of fluff that hardly anyone actually cares about.

Wait—what?

Did you have trouble reading that sentence? I would. Let's rewrite it:

Avoid unnecessary words.

As Hemingway once wrote, "If I started to write elaborately, or like someone introducing or presenting something, I found that I could cut that scrollwork or ornament out and throw it away and start with the first true simple declarative sentence I had written."[33]

Sometimes fewer words say more. Especially when our communication becomes wordy and confusing because we're nervous about what we're saying. Anxiety often causes us to over-explain.

---

[33] Ernest Hemingway. *A Moveable Feast: The Restored Edition*, Scribner, 2009, p. 22.

If you get nervous in high-stakes situations, as I often do, these books have helped me control my anxiety and communicate with more clarity:

- *Crucial Conversations* by Kerry Patterson
- *Radical Candor* by Kim Scott
- *Exactly What To Say* by Phil M. Jones
- *The Coaching Habit* by Michael Bungay Stanier

Is using fewer words always better? Not necessarily.

Joe Bunting of The Write Practice shows us how making a sentence longer—because you've added specificity—can make it much better.

Sentence 1: "She laughed loudly."

Sentence 2: "Her loud laugh seemed to reverberate through the party like a gong. Heads turned to see where the ruckus came from."

Which sentence is more descriptive? Which is more interesting?

The goal isn't brevity for its own sake—but rather clarity.

You have an idea in your head, and you want your readers to see that idea the way you do. Sometimes words help; but sometimes they get in the way. Reading a lot, and writing a lot, are the two activities I've found that help me know when to use more, and when to use less. Or, you could use hemingwayapp.com, a free resource that helps you write more like Hemingway.

My coauthor Aaron Wrixon also recommends Grammarly. You may have seen their ads targeted at new writers, Aaron says, but don't be fooled—even the experts love using Grammarly as an artificial intelligence-enabled proofreader and editor.

HOMEWORK

Examine your last post on LinkedIn.

Are there words you could cut to make it more clear?

Are there words you could *add* to make it more clear?

Now look at your bio and ask the same questions.

EXTRA CREDIT

Post this:

> *What has helped you be more clear in your communication with others?*
>
> *I'm looking for book recommendations, tips based on your own experience, or anything else you want to pass along.*
>
> *Thanks!*

DAY 50

AVOID ADVERBS (MOSTLY)

Regardless of what you think of Stephen King, you can't deny the man knows how to write and sell a lot of books, so when he says "The road to hell is paved with adverbs," it would be wise to at least consider what he means.

(Sidenote: I don't like *any* of King's books, except for *On Writing*, which is half biography, half writing advice, and it's FANTASTIC. Best book I've ever read on the craft of writing.)

However, if you can't trust King on anything, then try this quote from Mark Twain:

"Adverbs are the tool of the lazy writer."

But what are adverbs, anyway, and why are they so bad?

An adverb is a word that modifies or describes an adjective, a verb, or another adverb.

Surprisingly fast. *Slowly* moving. *Very* carefully.

Spot the adverbs? Yes, they often end in "ly." Not always, though—"very" is used as an adverb there, too.

Commonly used adverbs include:

- Commonly
- Always
- Often
- Mostly

It is definitely (!) hard to avoid adverbs. Then again, eliminating adverbs isn't the point—the goal is to avoid using them too often. ("Too" is also an adverb.)

Adverbs I use too often include:

- Very
- Really
- Just
- Actually
- Truly

I'm going to be honest with you. The ability to constantly (!) police our writing for things like adverbs is beyond the reach of most of us. In truth, it was my coauthor Aaron Wrixon, a professional copywriter and editor, who scrubbed this book of most of them.

So what's an "amateur" writer to do?

Here's an easy rule of thumb—whenever you find yourself using a word to describe *how* someone does or did something, write down what they did instead. For example:

> She looked at him longingly.

vs.

> She looked at him, unblinking, unable to turn away. She longed to talk to him, for him to hold her hand, for things to be the

> way they were—even though that could never be, because now he was a turtle.

Which is more powerful? (Putting aside your feelings about turtles and magical transformations, of course.)

Replace your adverbs with an explanation of what the adverb means and you'll create compelling, powerful writing.

HOMEWORK

Check your profile to make sure you're not using any adverb that isn't 100 percent necessary.

Then, write a LinkedIn post. Write without thinking about adverbs at first. Then review it to see if it has any, and try to eliminate them.

EXTRA CREDIT

Post this, as a token of the last time you will use unnecessary adverbs on your profile:

> *My job is very, very, very . . . [give your answer].*
>
> *Because . . . [again, your answer].*

DAY 51

LAUNCH A LINKEDIN NEWSLETTER

In 2019, LinkedIn introduced newsletters, which are like a series of articles or blog posts that people can subscribe to. Whenever you publish a new newsletter, your subscribers get a notification. It's a way to build an audience and get more eyes on your content.

Unfortunately, not everyone has access to create LinkedIn newsletters. LinkedIn says they are "in the process of slowly rolling out the ability to create newsletters to members globally . . ."[34] but I've heard rumors that LinkedIn won't be expanding access to the tool—if you don't already have it, you most likely won't get it in the future. To check whether or not LinkedIn will let you create a newsletter, go to your LinkedIn homepage and click "Write an article" at the top. If LinkedIn has granted you access to author a newsletter, you'll see "Create a newsletter" as an option.

To create a great LinkedIn newsletter:

1. **Choose a great name.** Arianna Huffington can get away with calling hers *My Weekly Thoughts* because she's uber-famous,

---

[34] See https://www.linkedin.com/help/linkedin/answer/97500/newsletters-on-linkedin-faq. Accessed 16 September 2021.

while author Nir Eyal, who is slightly less famous, chose a more descriptive newsletter name: *The Latest on Business, Behavior, and the Brain.*

2. **Write a great description.** After your newsletter name, your next chance to hook subscribers is the brief description that accompanies it. Bob Glazer's newsletter, *#Elevate*, "focuses on leadership, building capacity, and reaching potential." Rachel Botsman's newsletter, *Rethink with Rachel,* focuses on "Teaching people how to think, not what to think."

3. **Share your newsletter page.** There is no central directory of all the LinkedIn newsletters. You can't find them through LinkedIn search. You can't even Google them. People can only subscribe to your newsletter if it pops up as a suggestion under Network, or if they go to one of your articles and click the "Subscribe" button. Unfortunately, "subscribe" isn't that prominent. For that reason, it's important to make it easy for people to find your newsletter page by linking to it from the Featured section on your profile and in your About section, and also promote it through your non-LinkedIn channels like your personal brand website, email newsletter, or other social media accounts.

4. **Post regularly.** Post every day if you can, but weekly, bi-weekly, or monthly will be a more reasonable rhythm for most. The biggest mistake many newsletter authors make is they give up and stop. Slow and steady wins the race.

5. **Include a call to action.** Without a call to action, or CTA, subscribers will read your newsletter, say, "That was interesting," and never think about it again. However, if you include a CTA that asks them to leave a comment, share your newsletter, or click on a link, many of them will. Every time

you create a newsletter, ask yourself what you want them to do after they read it, and then invite them to do it.

Q: What if I don't have the ability to author a newsletter?

First, don't feel bad. I don't have it, and I know of other LinkedIn content creators who have hundreds of thousands of followers and have created great content for years, and they never got it either.

I hope the rumors I've heard aren't true, and that we'll all get newsletters someday, but if we don't, newsletters are still a great way to connect with those who have them. It's one more opportunity to reach out and say, "Hey, I love what you said in your last newsletter . . ." and forge a relationship. Not to mention, some newsletters contain great content that is worth your while to read!

HOMEWORK

Go to your LinkedIn homepage and click "Write an article" at the top to see if you have "Create a newsletter" as an option.

If you've got it, launch a newsletter! If you don't have it, find a LinkedIn newsletter you're interested in and subscribe to it so you're familiar with how it works and what type of content you like. And make sure to reach out and tell the author how much you like it!

EXTRA CREDIT

Here's your post for the day:

> *Are you subscribed to any LinkedIn newsletters you love? Which ones and why?*

DAY 52

SHARING IS CARING, BUT . . .

If LinkedIn had a setting for posts that would disable sharing, I'd use it on every single post I create.

"Wait, I thought social media was all about sharing. What do you mean I shouldn't encourage it?"

You're right, sharing is normally a wonderful thing on social media, but not when it comes to LinkedIn posts. (Note: This does not apply to articles.) When you create a post and someone shares it, they effectively create a new post. If people then comment on *that* post, the comments won't show up on your post—only on theirs.

But you want attention on *your* original post, of course, not someone else's!

Don't get me wrong—it isn't *harmful* if someone shares your post. You should be grateful for the thought, and the number of shares is a sign of how much people like your post. However, it isn't as helpful as if they were to comment on your original post and tag a few of their friends to come look at it.

How do you politely discourage sharing? You don't. Don't discourage sharing, but don't encourage it either. If you want to keep attention on your post, then first—and most obviously—don't *ask* your audience to share it.

Second, encourage people to comment on your post by asking good, open-ended questions. In addition, ask for comments and ask your audience to tag people "in the comments below." In every way, point your audience towards the comments section of your own post.

Lately, you may have commented on someone else's post, only to notice a note from LinkedIn that says, "Lead the conversation by turning your comment into a post." Even though LinkedIn now encourages sharing posts, it's generally better to comment. However, if you feel compelled to share someone else's post, follow these steps, shared with me by Lorri Randle, a LinkedIn expert with Pneuma Consulting:

1. Add 150+ of your own words when you share the post.
2. Add three unique hashtags (don't repeat any that are in the original post).
3. Tag the author of the original post.
4. Make sure the original author comments on your post.
5. Respond to all comments within an hour after they're made.[35]

By following these steps, you will perform well, and you'll also be helping the person whose post you're sharing.

[35] Personal communication with Josh Steimle.

HOMEWORK

Create a new post on LinkedIn and encourage your audience to engage with you in the comments.

EXTRA CREDIT

Post this:

> *When do YOU share vs. like vs. comment on a post?*
>
> *I will share if . . . [give your reason].*
>
> *For me, I like a post if . . . [give your reason].*
>
> *I will comment if . . . [give your reason].*
>
> *What about you?*

DAY 53

STAY ACTIVE

The same advice given to our senior citizens applies to LinkedIn. Staying active is the key to "staying alive" on the social network.

Each time you "like" something on LinkedIn, this activity shows up on your profile and in your feed. The same thing happens when you comment on a post, or create a new one.

Note: Update whether or not people can see your activity on LinkedIn in Settings & Privacy by clicking on "Visibility." I recommend you set it so everyone can see your activity.

Active profiles get more attention. Inactive profiles don't show up in people's feeds, so they only show up in searches. (That is, assuming they're not intentionally filtered out in Sales Navigator searches that specify "profiles active in the last thirty days" nor in LinkedIn Recruiter searches that specify "most likely to respond").

Even when it comes to a normal search, which profiles do you think LinkedIn is more likely to show first in searches—those that are active, or those that are inactive?

How active is active enough?

Liking a single post once a month is enough to keep you in those filtered Navigator searches, but the more you're active, the more you'll show up. Find a schedule that works for you, but try to do at least one thing on LinkedIn each week, whether it's posting or commenting.

HOMEWORK

For the next week, substantially increase your activity on LinkedIn. See if you notice a positive bump in your profile views and engagement on your posts.

EXTRA CREDIT

Post this, and watch how many people respond. This may be your most popular post yet.

> *Here are some of the most active commenters on my posts, and I want to publicly thank them for taking time from their schedules to engage. I appreciate the discussions we've had and the insights you've shared with me.*
>
> *[Tag ten to twenty people who have commented on your recent posts.]*

DAY 54

CREATE A ROUTINE

The right LinkedIn routine for you may be different than mine, but here's what mine looks like:

I have a to-do list for each day.

Posting to LinkedIn is a priority on that list.

I keep all my LinkedIn posts in Google Docs, and each day, as I get to "Post to LinkedIn" on my to-do list, I open my document full of LinkedIn posts and I create the text for the next post.

Then, I post it.

And now, because I'm already on LinkedIn, I check notifications. Any comments on my posts? LinkedIn messages? Connection requests? Check, check, check.

By the time I'm done, I've created new content, I've kept older content active, I've communicated with a bunch of people, and added new connections to my network.

I generally do this five days a week and often check LinkedIn multiple times each day, but sometimes I get busy. However, at a minimum, I go through this routine and it keeps me active on LinkedIn—and gets me great results without taking more than a few minutes each day.

HOMEWORK

Create a LinkedIn routine for this week. Stick to it, but don't be afraid to modify it if you think of something better. Then, once that week's done, try another week—until you've developed the habit.

EXTRA CREDIT

Post this for some social accountability.

> *I'm trying to build a new LinkedIn habit where I get on the platform every day. If you haven't seen me in a while, call me out!*
>
> *What about you—do you have a LinkedIn routine?*

SECTION 5

PLAY THE LONG GAME

When I was a kid, my dad gave me the weekly task of mowing the front and back lawns of our house. He challenged me to find satisfaction in a job well done.

One day, I heard a story about a young boy working on a farm, plowing fields, who was reprimanded by an older farmer for leaving crooked furrows as he plowed. "I can't help it!" the boy said. "No matter how careful I am, no matter how much I look at what I'm doing, I can't keep the plow straight!"

"*That's* your problem," the old farmer said, "You're looking at what you're doing, rather than where you're going."

The farmer continued, "Instead of looking down at your plow and the ground, choose something far away in the distance, beyond the field. Keep your eye on it as you plow."

The boy tried the old farmer's advice, and when he got to the end of a row and looked back, the furrow he had left behind him was perfectly straight.

I tried this out while mowing the lawn, and it worked for me, too! From then on, I had perfectly straight lines whenever I mowed.

On LinkedIn, looking beyond the short term and expanding your vision will help you chart a more direct course to the results you want. In this section, I share some of the tools, practices, and principles that will help you use LinkedIn effectively now, and for years to come, even as LinkedIn changes.

DAY 55

TRY THE TOOLS

There are a lot of LinkedIn tools and options we haven't covered in this book, and by next year, there will be even more. Some tools will stay, and others will go (like LinkedIn Stories). Regardless, you'll benefit if you try them all out because when one comes along that's particularly valuable, you'll be among the first to benefit and ride the wave.

Below are some of the tools my coauthors and I recommend.

SALES NAVIGATOR

Should you pay for an enhanced version of LinkedIn?

The answer depends on what you plan to use LinkedIn for. If you want to engage in thought leadership on LinkedIn and be a power user, then yes, I recommend you upgrade to Sales Navigator. (There are other paid versions, but for me, this is the one that packs the most punch.)

Here are two of the reasons I use it:

1. InMails: These are the LinkedIn private messages that allow you to contact anyone without an introduction or contact information—and with Sales Navigator, you get twenty per month. This is how I got through to almost half the CMOs I

interviewed for my book, *Chief Marketing Officers at Work*, after all other efforts failed.

2. More search: If you have an unpaid account and perform a search, you get limited search results. With Sales Navigator, you get much more. That means I can make more meaningful connections, faster.

Both of these benefits are well worth the price. If you don't know why you're buying Sales Navigator, then it's expensive—but if you want to make thousands of meaningful connections quickly and engage in thought leadership, then it's cheap at any price.

LINKEDIN POLLS

When you start a new LinkedIn post, there is an option to create a poll. When I was finalizing this book, I used a poll to decide on the title. I wasn't sure whether it should be "LinkedIn Mastery" or if I should include the lessons or days in it and call it "60 Days to LinkedIn Mastery." I created a one-day poll, and 405 votes later, there was a clear winner. Seventy-five percent of those who responded said the title *60 Days to LinkedIn Mastery* would hook their attention better and encourage them to take a closer look.

COMPANY PAGES

Not too long ago, company pages were largely a waste of time (except that creating one meant a company logo, rather than a gray placeholder, would show up next to your relevant work experience on your profile). Recently, LinkedIn added features and gave them enhanced prominence, making them more valuable. If you have a company, create a company page on LinkedIn and begin using all the features to connect your team, publish content, and attract new talent and customers.

OPEN TO . . .

If you're looking for a new job, activating the "Open to Work" setting can help employers and recruiters find you faster because it puts an easily recognized label on your LinkedIn photo. On the other hand, it can come across as slightly desperate and it also may warn your current employer that you're looking for work elsewhere, so use it with care.

If you're an employer, activate "Open to Hire" to show that you're looking for talent. The warning here is you may be swamped with applicants.

With both settings, it's easy to change so try one and switch back if it isn't working for you.

FUTURE TOOLS

In March, 2021, LinkedIn revealed that it was working on a feature, currently dubbed LinkedIn Audio, to rival the popular app Clubhouse, which allows participants to join "rooms" and communicate by voice.[36] As of this printing, the feature hasn't been released, but when it is, you'll be able to find quick access to it along with any other new tools in my free Ultimate LinkedIn Mastery Resource List at BlueMethod.io/list.

HOMEWORK

Check out the tools listed above, and see if any of them may be the right fit for you or your company.

---

[36] Sarah Perez. "LinkedIn confirms it's working on a Clubhouse rival, too." *TechCrunch*. 30 March 2021. Accessed 16 September 2021. https://techcrunch.com/2021/03/30/linkedin-confirms-its-working-on-a-clubhouse-rival-too.

EXTRA CREDIT

Post this:

> *Do you use a paid version of LinkedIn—and is it worth it?*
>
> *How has it been helpful for you?*

DAY 56

WATCH FOR PEOPLE SAYING THESE THINGS—IT MEANS YOU'RE DOING IT RIGHT

When you're engaging in thought leadership on LinkedIn—and doing it the right way, people will tell you things like:

- I feel like I know you!
- I see you everywhere!
- You're on fire!
- You seem to be doing really well!
- Can you help me do what you're doing?

If people feel like they know you, you're halfway to pulling them into your network because people do business with people they know, like, and trust.

If they see you everywhere, that means you have credibility in their eyes. You're an expert.

You'll attract more connections if you seem to be doing well because people are drawn to work with successful people.

The ultimate measure of your success as a thought leader is when someone wants your advice on how to do what you're doing. They want to be like you, do what you're doing, and get the results you're getting, and they recognize the only way to get what they want is to work with you.

HOMEWORK

Think about how to build credibility in other people's eyes. What one thing can you do on LinkedIn today to help build credibility?

EXTRA CREDIT

Post this:

> *Who are some people you've never met in real life but you feel like you know because of LinkedIn?*
>
> *Maybe you've never even communicated with them directly, but you read what they post—and it's so good you feel as though they were a trusted friend.*
>
> *For me, it's . . . [tag a few people you've never met in person, but you feel like you know all the same].*

DAY 57

STEP BACK AND REVIEW

I'm not a fan of paralysis by analysis, but a sensible amount of analysis can help us make better decisions about the future and achieve the success we're after. How do *you* define success?

In early 2019, I began to create graphics with LinkedIn tips to post on my Instagram account. Each graphic contained a quick LinkedIn tip. In the description accompanying the image, I provided more details. I wanted to see if there was an audience there who might be interested in my agency's LinkedIn services.

I didn't have any idea how many tips I wanted to create when I started, but a handful became ten, then twenty, then thirty, until at sixty tips I forced myself to stop.

Did the experiment work?

Not exactly. I couldn't get any traction on Instagram, no matter what I tried. Nobody on Instagram seemed to be interested in LinkedIn.

However, since I already had the graphics, I also posted them on LinkedIn. They didn't get a ton of attention, but as the days went on, there was enough interest to motivate me to keep going. Once I had written sixty, I realized I had enough content to put a book together—*this* book.

I announced my intention on LinkedIn, and a company reached out to ask if I would like to validate my book idea using their pre-sale/crowdfunding platform for authors. I posted a description of my book idea on their platform and started the campaign. Thirty days later, I had pre-sold 605 copies for a total of $26,441. It was one of the best-performing campaigns ever on the platform. Even better, it attracted the attention of multiple publishers.

Although my original plan to find LinkedIn clients through Instagram didn't work out, when I step back and look at what happened as a result, I'm glad I didn't give up too soon.

When you look at the results of any individual day since you started reading this book, you may or may not be able to point to any one change that made it all worth it. However, where are you today, in terms of using LinkedIn and the results you're getting, compared to when you started reading this book?

HOMEWORK

Revisit your purpose for being on LinkedIn by doing the following:

1. Record what your original purpose for being on LinkedIn was.
2. Make a list of ways you've made progress toward achieving your purpose since you started reading this book.
3. Write down any thoughts about how your purpose has changed since you started reading this book.
4. Create new goals. (A goal is a dream with a deadline.)
5. Prioritize your goals.
6. Define the actions that will complete each goal.
7. Narrow it down to the one action you will complete today.

8. Be flexible about where this work will take you. Don't be afraid to pivot or to embrace the success you achieve—even if it doesn't look the way you thought it would.

EXTRA CREDIT

Here's your post for today:

> *What's your big, hairy, audacious goal? The one you're afraid to share, because people might think you're crazy?*
>
> *The funny thing is, once you share your big vision, the world often comes together to help you make it happen. I've seen this is especially true on LinkedIn.*
>
> *Mine is . . . [share yours].*
>
> *What's yours?*

DAY 58

TEACH OTHERS HOW TO USE LINKEDIN

There's a viral quote on the internet, incorrectly attributed to Ben Franklin (among others), that says, "Tell me and I forget. Teach me and I may remember. Involve me and I learn." Perhaps the best way to get involved and develop true mastery of a subject is to teach it to others. This is backed up by modern-day research.

A 2014 study showed that "the act of teaching (i.e., by explaining the material to others) . . . is important for long-term learning,"[37] while a 2018 study demonstrated that, "Teaching . . . others enhances the teacher's own learning."[38]

As I mentioned on Day 37, you don't have to know more than everyone else in order to teach—you only need to know more than

---

[37] Logan Fiorella & Richard E. Mayer. "Role of Expectations and Explanations in Learning and Teaching." *Contemporary Educational* Psychology 39, no. 2 (2014): 75–85. Accessed 29 September 2021. https://www.sciencedirect.com/science/article/abs/pii/S0361476X14000022.
[38] Aloysius Wei Lun Koh et al. "The Learning Benefits of Teaching." *Applied Cognitive Psychology* 32, no. 3 (2018): 401–410. Accessed 29 September 2021. https://onlinelibrary.wiley.com/doi/abs/10.1002/acp.3410?campaign=wolearlyview.

your audience. However little you feel you know about LinkedIn, there are thousands of people who know less than you do. That means you can help them.

As you help others, you'll become more analytical in your thinking. You'll create experiments, you'll study, and you'll learn more about LinkedIn than I or anyone else can teach you.

"But I'm not out to become a LinkedIn expert," you say.

Then don't teach others about LinkedIn, teach them whatever you're an expert at (i.e., your genius zone). However, don't be afraid to sprinkle in LinkedIn tips here and there, because you are now a LinkedIn expert and can easily make LinkedIn part of your genius zone. Perhaps you started this book as "The patent law guy," but now you're "The patent law guy who's killing it on LinkedIn." Or maybe you were the "How to get a job in HR gal," but now you're the "How to use LinkedIn to get a job in HR gal."

Even a small amount of teaching others what you now know about LinkedIn will go a long way towards your own mastery.

HOMEWORK

Find one person to help with LinkedIn. It could be your spouse or significant other, a family member, or friend. Or use the extra credit post below to find someone. Offer to assist them using what you now know about LinkedIn.

EXTRA CREDIT

With this post, find someone to help:

> *Can I help you use LinkedIn better?*
>
> *I'm almost finished reading* 60 Days to LinkedIn Mastery, *a book about how to use LinkedIn better, and I've learned a ton. If you've got questions about*

LinkedIn, post them in the comments below and I'll do my best to answer them. Anything goes.

DAY 59

FOCUS ON WHAT NEVER CHANGES

Thirty thousand years ago, cavemen painted on the walls of caves to talk about what was important to them. They made pictures that tell us about their lives, food, and other things that were important to them.

Today, we post on social media. We talk about our lives, food, and other things that are important to us.

The fundamentals haven't changed—only the channel. We used to communicate with pictures on cave walls. Then we used stone tablets, metal plates, papyrus, parchment, and books.

Newspapers became the dominant mode of mass communication, followed by radio, TV, and, finally, the internet. (Which, by the way, isn't just one channel—it's millions, maybe even billions.)

The channels are always changing. What will we be using thirty thousand years from now? Who knows? We're not even sure what we'll be using a year or two from now. (Remember Friendster, MySpace, and Google+? And who had heard of TikTok a few years ago?)

While LinkedIn is an important channel, the channel doesn't matter as much as the content, so focus first on great content. Build your platform on an understanding of the psychology of your audience. Build it by growing relationships, one-on-one, with real people. LinkedIn will most likely still be a powerhouse twenty years from now, but even if it isn't, by focusing on great content, you'll be prepared no matter what the future brings.

Focus on what never changes.

HOMEWORK

Look at what those you admire most on LinkedIn are sharing. What format is it in? Is it plain text, images, links, or video? What type of information are they sharing?

EXTRA CREDIT

Post this:

> *Even as LinkedIn evolves, some things never change. For example, the people I follow like [tag a few of your favorite content creators] keep creating great content. The format of the content might change, maybe it's writing one day and video the next, but the quality doesn't change.*
>
> *Who are some of the best content creators you follow on LinkedIn, and what do you like about their content?*
>
> *I like posts that . . . [talk about what you are drawn to].*
>
> *What about you?*

DAY 60

LOVE, AND SHOW IT

In my upcoming book, *The 7 Systems of Influence,* System 7 is Love.

Not romantic love, of course. This is the "love" that means sincerely wanting to help others and wanting what's best for them. It's good will. It's caring enough about people to ask yourself, "How can I help them succeed?"

If you want LinkedIn success, it isn't enough to have a vision. Knowing your unique selling points and zeroing in on your target audience won't solve all your problems. A content calendar won't save you. Collaborating with others won't do it on its own. If you do everything else right, but you don't have love—if you don't truly care for the well being of those you serve—your efforts will fall flat.

It's like the conversation I had once with my business partner Corey Blake. We were talking about parenting and he said, "If your kids know you love them, it covers up a lot of mistakes."

If you do everything else wrong, but you've got love, you'll still win.

If you do everything else right, but you don't have the love, you'll still lose.

Revisit your purpose for being on LinkedIn. Is your purpose serving you, or serving others?

When you think about your genius zone, do you think about how to use it to give, or how to use it to get?

Do you truly care about your audience, or are you trying too hard to get them to care about you?

Without love, every action is merely a transaction. With love, actions gain meaning.

If your actions are motivated by love, it will show. And you'll achieve more on LinkedIn than you could ever imagine.

HOMEWORK

Stephen R. Covey, author of *The 7 Habits of Highly Successful People,* said that "Love is a verb."

What he meant is that love isn't just a feeling that magically appears. It's something that develops as you serve.

If you're not sure you love your audience, try serving them—not to make money, but just for the sake of serving them—and see what happens.

Go ahead. Find someone who is part of your audience and help them for free, without asking for anything in return. It can be something super easy and quick.

Do it, and see what happens.

EXTRA CREDIT

Post this:

> *Stephen R. Covey, author of* The 7 Habits of Highly Successful People, *said that "Love is a verb."*

What does that mean for you when you think about your customers, clients, partners, and team members?

CONCLUSION

You've now learned how to use LinkedIn to:

1. Optimize your profile
2. Make high-quality, meaningful connections
3. Create compelling content

Take a moment to reflect on how far you've come. If you implemented each of the suggestions as you read this book, you're now part of an exclusive group of LinkedIn experts. You probably didn't read this book because you wanted to become a six-figure-earning LinkedIn consultant, but with the knowledge you now have, you could. Now, as you share and teach what you've learned about LinkedIn to others, you'll truly master LinkedIn.

Who do you know who would benefit from this book?

Was there a chapter that was particularly interesting or helpful to you? Who else might find that information interesting or helpful?

Find those who need what you now know about LinkedIn, share a tip with them, or share the entire book, and you'll not only serve someone else, but increase your own mastery of LinkedIn.

NEED MORE?

Whether you find yourself saying, "I need more of this!" or, "Can't someone do all this for me?" these handy resources will help you continue to improve your LinkedIn game.

The Ultimate LinkedIn List

Check out the ever-expanding Ultimate LinkedIn Mastery Resource List, which lists every LinkedIn book, tool, and top LinkedIn expert. Download it for free at BlueMethod.io/list.

LinkedIn Post Prompts

If you enjoyed the extra credit LinkedIn prompts, how would you like to get new prompts every week? It's the easiest way to know what to post on LinkedIn. Sign up at BlueMethod.io/post.

Additional LinkedIn Services

If you need an audit or rewrite of your LinkedIn profile, want someone to manage growing your connections quickly for you, or need a 100 percent customized content plan, reach out to my LinkedIn agency BlueMethod (BlueMethod.io) or contact one of my coauthors, whose links are in their bios.

Finally, thank you for reading this book. We wrote it to serve you. We hope it has helped and will continue to help you on your LinkedIn journey.

AFTERWORD

The power of LinkedIn isn't the technology, it's the people. Ryan Roslansky became CEO of LinkedIn in 2020, but he doesn't control the network—you do. You, me, and everyone else who uses it. LinkedIn has to serve us, otherwise we'll leave. However, in order for LinkedIn to serve us, we have to serve each other. Who wants to be in a place where everyone is trying to get something from you?

Unfortunately, there is an element of this on LinkedIn. You see it when:

- You accept a connection request, and then immediately receive a sales pitch
- Someone creates content that's all about themselves, their company, or their product
- People ask for favors, but never offer anything

When people take without giving, it infects a community. It starts as individuals feel they must protect themselves—they can't give too freely, or they'll lose everything they have. A scarcity mindset sets in, and they hold back. As they serve less, so do others. Soon, the cycle spirals downward until the community is abandoned.

A community can tolerate a certain amount of selfishness as long as it's small compared to the level of generosity. Happily, I see a lot of this on LinkedIn. I saw it when:

- During the start of the pandemic, someone retooled their factory to make masks and posted on LinkedIn asking where they could send a million of them
- Someone offered their consulting advice, freely, to those who needed it but couldn't pay
- Users came together to raise funds for a woman whose house had been destroyed in a natural disaster

And I see it every day when people share what they know, endorse one another's skills, and provide recommendations. LinkedIn is a special, different place, unlike any other. If you don't believe me, spend a few minutes on Twitter for comparison's sake.

When people give freely, it inspires others to do the same. People adopt an abundance mindset, and the cycle reinforces itself—as long as it has fuel.

LinkedIn is the engine, but without us, it can't do a thing. Are we, in our shortsightedness, taking what we can get right now and hoping we can make it on our own? Or are we working together to add the fuel LinkedIn needs to help us all get to where we want to go?

This book is a tool, and while I hope you use it to get what you want from LinkedIn, I hope what you want is not only to find a new job, grow your business, or find new partners, but that you'll also want to help others get what they need and want.

If my coauthors or I can be of any assistance to you in this, please connect with us on LinkedIn and let's work together to make it the best tool we can, not only to change our professional lives, but to change the world.

ABOUT THE AUTHORS

Josh Steimle is an entrepreneur, speaker, and author whose posts on LinkedIn have been seen millions of times. He's a TEDx speaker, and has written or appeared in more than three hundred articles in publications like *Fortune*, *Time*, *Forbes*, *Inc.*, *Mashable*, *TechCrunch*, and *Entrepreneur*. He's the founder of Blue Method (BlueMethod.io), a LinkedIn agency. He lives in Arizona with his wife, three children, and their dog and three guinea pigs. Follow him at JoshSteimle.com and on LinkedIn at https://www.linkedin.com/in/joshuasteimle.

Virginie Cantin is the creator of *LinkedIn BREAK-IN*, an online course for professional women who want to attract more career opportunities. Virginie has worked in digital marketing since 2013. She uses her knowledge to help women advertise and advance their career. She lives in Switzerland with her husband and daughter. Find her at VirginieCantin.com and on LinkedIn at https://www.linkedin.com/in/virginie-cantin.

Andy Foote is a *reassuringly expensive* LinkedIn coach, and the founder of LinkedInsights.com. He created the Foote-Notes podcast last year and since being granted access to LinkedIn Live, has focused on finding unique and innovative ways to maximize engagement with fun livestream shows like "*16 Questions*" and "*The Blinkety Blank Quiz Show*." He coauthored *LinkedIn Made Simple* with

Ryan Rhoten. Find him on LinkedIn at https://www.linkedin.com/in/andyfoote.

Lorri Randle is a digital media strategist passionate about finding connections between people, ideas, and strategies. She teaches her clients how to use LinkedIn to build real relationships, become thought leaders in their industry, and authentically connect with their audience. When not on LinkedIn, she is hanging out with her 4 kids or in the mountains training for her next ultramarathon. Find her on LinkedIn at https://www.linkedin.com/in/lorrirandle.

Kyle Weckerly is a certified grant writer, helping engineering consulting firms secure funding, as well as a ghostwriter and an author. All of these endeavors have been greatly enhanced through utilizing LinkedIn. He lives in Texas with his wife and two daughters. When he's not writing, or expanding his network through LinkedIn, he's working on another book and training for a half-marathon. Find him on LinkedIn at https://www.linkedin.com/in/kyleweckerlygrantwriter.

Ben Wise is a ghostwriter and LinkedIn agency owner who helps founders and executives communicate their stories in an authentic, humanizing way. With more than two hundred million views on content he's ghostwritten, his clients have gotten leads from Fortune 500 companies, media attention from top publications, and interest from both investors and top talent. He homeschools his kids, practices Muay Thai, and consumes ramen. Find him on LinkedIn at https://www.linkedin.com/in/benawise.

Aaron Wrixon, founder of WRIXON, has been paid for writing well over seven million words. That's the equivalent of nine copies of the King James Bible. Aaron has written for more than 120 different industries across the English-speaking world. He lives in Canada, surrounded by women—his wife, his two daughters, two dogs, and a bearded dragon. In his spare time, he reads, plays board games, writes music, enjoys television and movies, and listens to a lot of weird CDs. Find him online at wrixon.com and on LinkedIn at https://www.linkedin.com/in/aaronwrixon.

Made in the USA
Coppell, TX
29 August 2022

82239839R10146